For Barbara —
with christmas love
from Tom
(with some help from
Elorie's Daddy)

PHILADELPHIA
The Intimate City

PHILADELPHIA
The Intimate City

Gloria Braggiotti Etting

Photographs by James A. Drake

Introduction by Alexander Biddle

A Studio Book · THE VIKING PRESS · New York

Acknowledgments

This project would have been impossible for me without the help of many of my dear friends. To the following I owe special thanks because they gave so generously of their time and knowledge: Mrs. Alexander Biddle, Mr. David J. Crownover, Mr. Henry E. Gerstley, Mrs. Josiah Marvel, Mr. and Mrs. George Brooke Roberts, Miss Juliet E. Stacks, and Mr. Reeves Wetherill.

G. B. E.

Copyright © 1968 by Gloria Braggiotti Etting
All rights reserved
First published in 1968 by The Viking Press, Inc.
625 Madison Avenue, New York, N. Y. 10022
Published simultaneously in Canada by
The Macmillan Company of Canada Limited
Library of Congress catalog card number: 68-19323
Printed in U.S.A. by R. R. Heywood
Designed by Charles O. Hyman

CONTENTS

To Emlen, who brought me to Philadelphia

G. B. E.

For my mother and father

J. A. D.

INTRODUCTION

Ever since Colonial times, Philadelphia citizens in all walks of life have contributed their intelligence, hard work, skill, and wealth in carrying forward with quiet determination the work William Penn started after his accord with the Indians.

History books make much of the fact that it was in Philadelphia that the Declaration of Independence was signed, that the Constitution of the United States was drafted, and that the nation's first capital was established. Philadelphia was the home of the original publishing house, the first theater, the first art centers, the first zoo, and the first mint. In addition, the Franklin Institute is the country's oldest scientific organization. The Insurance Company of North America, the First Pennsylvania Banking and Trust Company, and the Philadelphia Saving Fund Society are also "firsts" in their particular fields, as is what is now the Philadelphia-Baltimore-Washington Stock Exchange.

The list is a long one, but I think it particularly significant today that the pioneering spirit astir two centuries ago should have renewed itself with such vigor. With commendable enthusiasm, our citizens have supported the visionary program of the Philadelphia Planning Commission. Miracles have already been performed in restoring whole streets of architectural treasures that had all but fallen into oblivion. At the same time, imposing new structures and highways have been built, which link our proud past with the present, and set an exemplary pace for the future.

Another important development has been the constructive approach to the unemployment problem. The Opportunities Industrialization Center, which was inaugurated in a converted Philadelphia jail, has trained over three thousand underprivileged citizens for jobs ranging from chefs to electronic technicians. The program has been so successful that sixty-five cities from New Haven to Los Angeles have begun developing similar centers.

We can also be proud of our contributions to medicine through our universities, our five great hospitals, and the three large drug concerns that spend some seventy-five-million dollars annually on medical research. Recently launched under the leadership of Dr. Gaylord Harnwell, the distinguished scientist who is now president of the University of Pennsylvania, and with the support of the Philadelphia business community, is the University Science Center.

In the world of music we have also been more fortunate than most communities. The Philadelphia Orchestra under the direction of Leopold Stokowski and Eugene Ormandy has, over the past forty years, become not only a national but also an international institution. Its home, the Academy of Music, has acoustics that are, perhaps, second to none, a fact which influenced the decision to renovate its home rather than to tear it down and rebuild, as is now the popular practice.

As in any city, we who live in Philadelphia associate it most intimately with the roots of childhood, with families and friends who have grown up in and around the original "greene countrie towne" which Penn mapped out between the banks of its two rivers. Although it has grown into the vast metropolis we see today, with busy shopping streets, factories, rows upon rows of houses, and the largest group of distinguished schools and colleges in the country (with the possible exception of Boston), inwardly the spirit of the city has changed little.

Gloria Braggiotti Etting has written about Philadelphia with the touch of an experienced journalist in love with the life of the city. She first saw it with the eyes of a stranger, and then during the thirty years she has lived here, first in Haverford, then in the city itself, with the vision of a glamorous, popular hostess. Recently Gloria commented that the people she met when she first came to Philadelphia have remained her best friends. If we apply modern analytics to this, the answer is that her husband Emlen, an artist who knew everyone in town, had planned her entrance to Philadelphia with an intelligent view to the future.

This book is a valuable addition to the folklore of Philadelphia, in which so much interest has developed in recent years and about which much has been written. What distinguishes the book especially is the element implied in the subtitle — the intimacy of the city as a place to live in and to work. Philadelphia and many of its prominent citizens are presented here with warmth and affection, in the words of a Florentine who married a Philadelphian and fell in love with her new home. They are also presented pictorially by James A. Drake, a talented young native Philadelphian whose photographs, taken especially for the book, complement Gloria Etting's own album, which appears on the last few pages.

A number of the faces to be seen are not only familiar to Philadelphians, but to the world at large, for Philadelphia has given birth to statesmen, writers, artists, architects, musicians, and actors — to an extent that stimulated The Viking Press to publish these commentaries on our city.

Philadelphia is a way of life. It is steeped in tradition, yet has a concern for the future. The Quaker origins are still strong, yet all religions are practiced here; we have the background that attracts every kind of cultural endeavor, and the taste to appreciate rather than merely exploit music, art, and literature. If our pace is more leisurely than is found in some other cities, it is perhaps because we enjoy the way we set about getting things done.

ALEXANDER BIDDLE

THE INTIMATE CITY

During the thirty years I have lived in Philadelphia, watching it spread, develop, increase its population and prosperity, I have never known it to lose its sense of intimacy, its friendliness, its good manners. For these qualities alone, I love it.

Philadelphians, moreover, take the Greek implication of its name, city of "Brotherly Love," seriously. Taxi drivers open doors for you when you get in and out of their cabs; street cleaners smile "Good day" when you pass them along your block; policemen usually act as if they want to help rather than reprimand you; neighbors accept packages for you if nobody's home, and sales people in the largest department stores, even during the pre-Christmas stampedes, act humanely. Certainly not all the citizens are Quakers, yet without wishing to toss too many bouquets at the feet of its founding fathers, it must be said that Philadelphia really *is* a city of friends.

Unlike most big cities — and Philadelphia is the fourth largest in the United States — I have never heard of a visitor who has complained of being lonely or feeling a sense of anonymity there. In fact, the atmosphere is so relaxed that when I first arrived here in 1938, Philadelphia seemed more like a large "small city" than one of America's great centers, once its capital and still a leader in industry, science, law, medicine, education, and music.

On my first drive through Philadelphia, I circled excitedly round City Hall, the great landmark with the benevolent figure of William Penn at the top. From this, Philadelphia's central and most visually prominent building, it is an easy walk to most of the important shops, and on my very first expedition I already had a feeling of contact. I felt lost only when, out of habit, after ten years of Manhattan, I zigzagged hurriedly through the crowds or jay-walked through the congestion of traffic. Unlike New Yorkers, Philadelphians simply do not feel impelled to get there fast, furiously, and *first*. People go about their business quietly and pleasantly as if they belonged to the city and the city to them.

Ever since 1681 when William Penn founded the Quaker City, serenity has meant "still strength" — an undaunted capacity for self-control. This my mother-in-law brought home to me when she told about her aunt, Adelaide Fury. Returning from a ball one evening, "Aunt Addie" opened her wardrobe to hang up her gown, and discovered a burglar crouched between the frills and laces. She looked him straight in the eye and with unflinching composure said: "Hadn't thee better get thee to thy little home?" and — dumfounded — he did!

It is an unwritten Philadelphia law that no other city building shall rise higher than the rim of Billy Penn's hat on the City Hall statue. While new apartment houses, offices, and bank buildings have sprung up in strategic locations, except for the new Philadelphia Saving Fund Society building, they have left a clear view of the founding father. This statue, standing thirty-seven feet high, was cast in bronze from a model by Alexander Milne Calder, eldest of three generations of famous Philadelphia artists. His son Alexander Stirling Calder created the heroic figures for the fountains in the center of Logan Square, while grandson Alexander Calder, internationally famous creator of mobiles and stabiles, is best represented here by his gigantic "Ghosts," which flutters over the grand staircase in the Philadelphia Museum of Art. And now a fourth generation, Alexander's daughter Sandra, is a successful book illustrator. Alexander Calder's works are treasured by collectors all over the world, as are those of other famed citizens from Benjamin West to Andrew Wyeth, who now lives at Chadds Ford, a pleasant drive out of the city.

In scanning Philadelphia's skyline from Fairmount Park, you would not, today, be aware of Penn's plan for a green city with equidistant parks from river to river. However, his idea was to arrange the city around five green squares. From Center Square (now City Hall), the streets running north and south were given numbers, while those running east and west all the way from Pine to Cherry Street were named after native Philadelphia trees. Penn granted lots in the city or in the suburbs to anyone who took up a grant of the country acreages beyond the city, with a view to creating an interdependence between town and country.

Penn's "greene countrie towne" — what is left of it — can be seen most clearly when you fly into Philadelphia and look down at the squares nestling like emerald jewels in a framework of steel, brick, and cement. Despite Philadelphia's booming urban development and its wide-reaching suburbs, the main charm of the city still lies in these green oases and the many residential streets that are to be found in reconstructed Society Hill or around Rittenhouse Square where houses retain the character of the early city or have been tastefully restored in the best Philadelphia tradition.

I remember how animated Leopold Stokowski became on the subject of the city one evening at our house on Panama Street. The maestro was appearing in Philadelphia as a guest conductor. "You know," he said, raising his hand as if to lead the conversation into more personal channels, "I wonder if you people truly appreciate the unique charm of your city. . . ." One of his favorite relaxations was exploring the streets so reminiscent of London mews — Waverly, Addison, Van Pelt, Cypress, and others which, like rivulets, flow unpredictably from one block to another.

Not the least attractive of the "greenes" is Logan Square, or Logan Circle as it is usually called because of the circulating traffic merging there from many directions. It has often been compared to the Rond Point in Paris, although it is less chaotic. Dominating it is the main library, one of Philadelphia's forty public libraries, a building which, together with the County Court, forms an almost exact replica of Jacques-Ange Gabriel's twin buildings in the Place de la Concorde: the Hôtel Crillon and the Ministère de la Marine.

Another echo of Paris — of the Champs Élysées — is the handsome grass-bordered Benjamin Franklin Parkway, with its side lanes attractively shaded by trees. The mile-long drive is climaxed by the largest of Philadelphia's impressive Greek-revival buildings — the Philadelphia Museum of Art, which, like a golden Parthenon, sits majestically on top of a hill leading into Fairmount Park.

This area of Philadelphia not only shows the influence of Paris and of Greek architecture, but has touches of Italy and Holland too. Italy, in fact, often jumps to my mind — for the city's renaissance spirit reminds me of Florence, and so do the many artists and artisans who work here and like to use their creative talents in their own city.

Alexander Stirling Calder's fountain in Logan Square, with its three recumbent nude statues, reminds me of Rome's Piazza Navona. Calder's figures, representing Philadelphia's three rivers — an Indian, the industrialized Delaware; a mature woman, the confident Wissahickon; and a young woman, the sportive Schuylkill — recall not only the theme of Bernini's fountain symbolizing the rivers of the world, but also the Italian sculptor's sensuous poses, evoked in heroic proportions.

Holland's role in the Philadelphia scene is more ephemeral and recent. The riot of red, yellow, and white tulips around the fountain were a gift of Queen Juliana. At the time of the Marshall Plan, Arthur Kaufmann, then President of Gimbel Brothers, thought it more constructive in some cases to stimulate European exports instead of merely sending financial aid to our allies, as the government was doing. As a result Gimbels put on a Netherlands Fair. Dutch products were brought over by the first Dutch passenger ship to dock in our port in 1950, and the then Mayor Bernard Samuel invited the Queen and her Consort to the opening.

Prince Bernhard brought a gift of one hundred thousand bulbs and he was received at City Hall by the Mayor and the First City Troop in full regalia. The following spring Queen Juliana, who had come to Washington on official business, made a special trip to Philadelphia when the tulips were in bloom for the first time, their brilliant cups bowed as if in honor of her presence.

It is not accidental that parts of Philadelphia reflect the beauty of Paris. The French architect Jacques Auguste Gréber, in cooperation with a team of Philadelphians — Frenchborn Paul Philippe Cret, Clarence Zantzinger, and Charles Borie — was commissioned in 1907 to add touches of Napoleonic grandeur to the city. Gréber designed the Champs-Élysées-like Benjamin Franklin Parkway, and Paul Cret the Rodin Museum. In front of this stands a replica of the garden wall of the Rodin Museum in Meudon, the sculptor's birthplace. The sculptured doors, "The Gates of Hell," inspired by Rodin's reading of Dante, are the original castings. Inside the museum is the largest collection of the sculptor's work outside France — a donation of the late philanthropist Jules E. Mastbaum. The Philadelphia Museum of Art was designed by Clarence Zantzinger and Charles Borie, with Horace Trumbauer.

Facing the museum from the north is the mounted figure of Joan of Arc in gleaming gold by Fremiet. Paradoxically, this is the original of the monument; the second casting stands in the Place des Pyramides in Paris. The museum is now backed on the north side by the Philadelphian — said to be the largest apartment-house complex under one roof in the world — a vision that the museum's architects could never have dreamed would occur in the area.

In front of the museum, dominating the parkway, stands the elaborate fountain with its statue of George Washington astride his horse. Given to the city by the Society of the Cincinnati, it was cast from a mold for a statue of Frederick the Great, with the hat and the medals changed. Below are sculptured fountains depicting animals indigenous to the area in the General's time. Below the west entrance is an equestrian fountain in travertine copied from one in the Borghese Gardens and presented to the city by Mussolini.

A very different side of Philadelphia is to be found in Washington Square at Sixth and Walnut Streets, where many people start their tour of the city. The square has a sleepy poetic charm, as though it had refused to be influenced by encroaching "progress." Old people, enjoying benches shaded by plane and horse chestnut trees, lift their faces to catch flickers of sunshine, unaware, probably, that this square was the burial ground for many soldiers of the American Revolution. Children skip playfully across the grass, pausing now and then to stare at the statue of George Washington (a replica of the one by Jean-Antoine Houdon

11

in Richmond), or at the monument to the Unknown Soldier of the American Revolution.

In the short time it takes to walk around the square, you can see several buildings of different historic interest: the first publishing house of the United States, Lea and Febiger (the original publishers of Edgar Allan Poe and Washington Irving); Saunders, publishers of the best-selling Kinsey reports on *Sexual Behavior in the Human Male* and *Sexual Behavior in the Human Female*; J. B. Lippincott Company, another of America's oldest and still most active publishing houses; the still-private Athenaeum Library; and the lovely Colonial-style brick house built in 1956 by former Mayor Richardson Dilworth, now President of the Board of Education.

On the north of Washington Square is the Curtis Publishing Company building, which used to house the editorial offices of the *Saturday Evening Post, Holiday,* and the *Ladies' Home Journal.* Hopkinson House, a skyscraper apartment building completed in 1962, massively dominates the quaintness of Washington Square.

The area around Franklin Square, the green block that greets everyone coming to Philadelphia across the Benjamin Franklin Bridge from New Jersey, is bursting with redevelopment. Its new architectural population — the Police Administration Building, the Independence Mall to the south, and the Metropolitan Hospital — replaces the flophouses and honkytonks of another day.

Even more than in most American cities, the buildings of Philadelphia stem from many periods and styles, and stand side by side and in different stages of preservation. I often think of it as a large, rambling old house filled with inherited or collected objects — some cherished and cared for, some neglected and unrepaired, others recently acquired, bright, shining, and modern. Philadelphia is a city of contrasts, some planned, some unplanned, but nearly always fitting comfortably together.

My favorite of Penn's squares is Rittenhouse Square, probably because I see it nearly every day and consider it the focal point of our neighborhood, but also because it is refreshing and well kept. Some years ago, the owners of the Eglin Garage had a first "quiet" hearing with the Philadelphia Zoning Board in an attempt to rush a permit through to excavate a garage under the square. This would have meant uprooting the flowering cherry and plane trees and pouring cement over the hallowed "greene." After getting wind of this plan, members of the Center City Residents Association, some five hundred of them, assembled at the YMCA on Chestnut Street for what proved to be a stormy meeting. Walter Hudson, who was manager of the Embassy Apartments and head of the Association, George Gordon Meade, Judge L. Stauffer Oliver, Fuery Ellis, well-known public service officer, and Philip Klein, delivered fiery speeches in which the "progressive" garage management was threatened with action following a proposed march on City Hall. Philip Klein is now President of Harcum Junior College. The others, regrettably, are gone, but the continued life of the square is a tribute to their memory.

I often think of that nightmare while strolling there; deriving even more pleasure, perhaps, from the familiar sight of people walking their dogs, children playing around the famous bronze goat or feeding peanuts to the squirrels in the lovely environment of trees, earth, and flowers, for the very reason that Rittenhouse Square came close to being stolen away from us.

My affection for the square — and all of Philadelphia — dates back to the days when Emlen and I used to have tea with his aunt, Mrs. John A. Brown, Jr., who lived during the winter at 224 South Nineteenth Street. Her Victorian limestone mansion, built in the florid renaissance style of the Château de Chambord, was one of the last on the square to be kept up in the grand manner of the days when almost every building around it was a private house. My husband recalls that she used to drive to Wanamaker's in a brougham. After Mrs. Brown died in 1941 her house was occupied for a while by the Italian Consulate, and then it was finally torn down to make way for the Dorchester Apartments, which now take up almost the entire block.

In spite of the huge apartments now overpowering the neighborhood in our own little city within a city, (sometimes referred to as Philadelphia 3, for our old postal zone number), famous people stroll about as peacefully and unobserved as Pearl Buck or her neighbor and friend, Dr. Isador Ravdin, one of the world's greatest surgeons and cancer specialists. Many doctors, in fact, live in our "little city," particularly in the neighborhood of Rittenhouse Square or Pine and Spruce Streets, where so many of the old mansions have been converted into medical offices. It is sometimes said that "in almost every prominent Philadelphia family there is always a doctor in the house."

If there is not a doctor, then there is often a member of the family on the board of one of the many hospitals, such as the Jefferson, the University of Pennsylvania Hospital, the Lankenau, the Bryn Mawr, the Presbyterian, the Children's, and, of course, the nation's first, the Pennsylvania Hospital. In no other city are there so many citizens who occupy so much time on board and committee meetings — another proof of how much heart goes into the city, its needs, and its progress.

Philadelphia is no different from any other modern city in giving way to the new order, except that its planners have now earned a world reputation as perhaps the most success- ful in restoring whole areas of historic buildings, and combining these with contemporary and modern architecture in a way that is both harmonious and functional. They have made an obvious effort to prevent the city from developing into the anonymity of a metropolis, even though it is growing at a staggering clip.

Drastic changes in living have not eliminated the character and charm of the late Georgian and early Victorian brick houses of DeLancey Place, occupied by such prominent Philadelphians as the Efrem Zimbalists, the Arthur Youngs, and architect George B. Roberts and his wife Mary (authors of *Triumph on Fairmount*). Even the DeLancey Place houses that have been divided into apartments have been beautifully maintained. Indeed, if you overlook the intrusions of the twentieth century — parked automobiles, housewives strug- gling home with bags of groceries, and the invasion of blue jeans and mini-skirts — you are back in the days when horse-drawn carriages drew up at those marble doorsteps. Out of those carriages would have stepped ladies dressed in long bustled skirts, making a great display of gloved hands that never peeled an onion, let alone polished a floor.

In the summer, to escape the heat, these fashionable ladies fled with their spouses — and servants — to the country, which to Philadelphians, to this day, means exclusively the Main Line, Germantown, and Chestnut Hill. The residents of DeLancey Place and Locust Street were the last to forsake their town houses and settle permanently in the "country." The less fortunate, whose town houses were on or near Pine, Spruce, Walnut, Chestnut, and Market Streets, were chased out by the invasion of shops. Today, with buses replacing trolley cars, the advent of air conditioning, and slum areas restored to Williamsburg-like perfection, the attractions of year-round life in town have brought many families back to the center of the city.

This movement, which began only a few years ago, coincided with Philadelphia's

"Renaissance." When the great team of Senator Joseph Clark and ex-Mayor Richardson Dilworth had the city's littered streets cleaned up, improved the unbearable drinking water, and induced the "independents" (mostly adamant Republicans) to shift their votes to the Democratic Party, town living began its greatest comeback.

The reaction of the English designer Peter Morris, recently in Philadelphia for the first time, is typical of most visitors. "It was love at first sight," he wrote. "I got the feeling of peace that I had not expected in such a great city . . . parts of Philadelphia appeared familiar to me . . . they reminded me of England and they were so lovingly taken care of by people who must really care. But most interesting is the combination of the industries raging at full tilt, the network of highways weaving through the city without interrupting the local traffic, skyscraping apartment houses and office buildings which fail to dominate Philadelphia's essential mood of serenity, and the cozy elegance of the small intimate streets. Some of it is good enough for a theatrical set."

SHRINES AND TRADITIONS

T he sight-seeing visitor or foreigner in any city is often better rehearsed about "what not to miss" than those who are a part of it, who take their treasures for granted and who have a *mañana-mañana* kind of attitude of putting off visiting today what they can see tomorrow. Philadelphians today, however, are experiencing an inner revaluation of their city which is in pace with the extraordinary face lifting that has been going on for the past several years.

Citizens are interested in seeing once again what is here and what belongs to them, not only to appreciate the magnitude of what happened when America first came into its own, but to enjoy and be proud of the intelligent way the city has cleaned away the slums that had grown like weeds around some of the most historic and beautiful buildings in the country.

At last, Independence Hall's brick structure breathes again, seen in the new perspective provided by the landscaped mall reaching all the way to Franklin Square. The spire gives the illusion of rising higher above the block of square buildings than it actually does, and the mall provides a feeling of space and quietness. At night, when the rows of lamps standing inside the park's low brick wall are lit, their globes look like suspended golden balloons — glowing as if to gladden the heart of every American. No matter from what part of the world they come, people cannot help being moved when they face Independence Hall, sanctuary of the message of liberty and freedom to all people. Here, and in the surrounding square mile, probably more Colonial treasures exist than can be found within similar walking distance anywhere else in America.

A plaque over the door outside Independence Hall reads: "The State House of Pennsylvania — the birthplace of the United States of America," and the interior, after many restorations, is almost exactly as it used to be. The steps have been rebuilt and some of the original brick, said to have been imported from England, was used to restore the inside as well as the exterior. All the original windows were preserved, and many of the beams have been skillfully reinforced. Among many authentic touches that bring the interior alive are the bottle-green cloths placed over the tables where the fifty famous men who once met here rested their elbows while writing, pondering, or pounding their fists. If books were strewn on the floor, or your nostrils were filled with the smell of snuff, or you could hear heated arguments swelling above the buzz of horseflies from neighboring stables, even less would be left to the imagination.

Congress Hall, which became a county court when America's capital was transferred to Washington, is also to be seen as it looked during its earliest days. The hall was restored in 1962 (for the third time) and was furnished by the National Park Service, complete with candles set on the desks, which are authentically placed in a semicircle.

It is not surprising that the architecture of many educational and business buildings throughout the United States should have been inspired by the beauty — and fame — of Independence Hall. The Menninger Foundation in Topeka, Kansas, is a modified version of it, as is a building for classrooms, offices, and chapel at Berea College, Kentucky. Baker Hall at Dartmouth College is not only similar to Independence Hall but also faces an open area much the same as the mall. The grand entrance of another "twin" sweeps up to the processing office in Macon, Georgia, of the Insurance Company of North America — appropriately, since the headquarters of this firm is in Philadelphia. Lowell House, a residence building for Harvard undergraduates in Cambridge, also copies the Hall in a more massive form, and in New York, the Kew Gardens Hills branch of the Queens County Savings Bank not only suggests Independence Hall but displays a replica of the Liberty Bell in the lobby.

It is estimated that over a million and a half visitors to Philadelphia view the Bell every year. This "Baby of Our Cradle of Independence" weighs 2800 pounds — a composite of copper, tin, and lead. In spite of the strong mineral compound, the condition of the Bell, which cracked when it tolled for Chief Justice John Marshall's funeral in July, 1835, had deteriorated to such a point that it took mechanical engineers from the Franklin Institute over a year to study the problem and find a satisfactory way of reinforcing it in 1962. Perhaps our Bell was never meant to ring for the dead, but for the living — and above all for an ideal. Although it is now mute, its echoes will never stop ringing in the hearts of men and women of the free world.

From Independence Hall, streets, lawns, and byways lead to a number of buildings that are historically, architecturally, and spiritually related. Christ Church burial ground, at Arch and Fifth Streets, has five signers of the Declaration of Independence resting under the shade of its tall trees. Marked "Benjamin and Deborah" is the grave of Franklin and his wife. Almost any time you pass there, you will see youngsters squeezing their faces between the iron bars of the cemetery, gaping with awe at the simple grave of the great man. The quiet churchyard has the aspect of a spacious, luxuriantly green park, and on days when it is open, strollers may pause and meditate, sit on a bench and munch a sandwich, or toss a penny for luck on Benjamin Franklin's gravestone.

Despite the fact that he was born in Boston, Benjamin Franklin looms as a friend whom every Philadelphian associates uniquely with his city. Next to Penn he is the city's "patron saint" for his contributions to science and to every branch of industry, education, medicine, and civics.

In true American tradition Benjamin Franklin began humbly as a printer at the age of seventeen and rose to the elevated plane of an emissary to France during the Revolutionary War. His image and name are scattered throughout the city like souvenirs of good will. The bridge connecting Philadelphia with Camden, New Jersey, as well as the parkway and the Franklin Institute are named after him; there are two statues of him (one as a youth newly arrived in the city, and one as a mature man) at the University of Pennsylvania, which he founded in 1740. The bronze statue by James Earle Fraser portrays the inventor, civic leader, and *bon vivant* as partly bald, and in the comfortable pose of a man who has reached his highest goals and can now enjoy watching his life's work continue to evolve. And there, larger than life, with kindly face, he appears ready to speak to and encourage every young

16

Opposite: Independence Hall, from Congress Hall.

Overleaf: Penn Center office buildings and City Hall.

student — generation after generation — at the college which, without his sagacity, would never have started on the way to its present high academic standing.

Despite his taste for good living and his great genius for civic and cultural reforms, judging by his haphazard way of dressing and his casual ways, he apparently had few social aspirations. While doing research for *Inside U. S. A.* John Gunther came to Philadelphia. At dinner one evening he asked a lady of the Biddle family who she thought was Philadelphia's leading citizen. "I don't know," she answered. "Suppose you had been asked this same question in 1770, would you have answered Benjamin Franklin?" the author pursued. "Oh, but he came from such an undistinguished family," exclaimed the Philadelphia socialite. But surely had Franklin cared to conquer Society he would have done so.

Visitors who come to Philadelphia merely for a pleasant social weekend, or to see special exhibitions such as the Manet show at the Philadelphia Museum of Art or the Andrew Wyeth show at the Academy of the Fine Arts (which attracted a greater attendance than any other one-man show in the Academy's history), now include a tour in and around Independence Hall — something they would never have thought of undertaking before the local renaissance. The tour includes, of course, Carpenter's Hall, the Second Bank of the United States, the American Philosophical Society, and usually a walk along cobbled Elfreth's Alley, one of the oldest inhabited streets in America, which has fortunately been preserved as it was in the eighteenth century. This tiny street, only twenty feet wide, runs from Front Street to Second Street, and between Arch and Race Streets, and its thirty-three houses were originally occupied by craftsmen. The street was named for Jeremiah Elfreth, who came to Philadelphia as a blacksmith in 1690.

As Mr. Van Day Truex, designer and former president of the Parsons School of Design in New York, has said, "I've been coming to Philadelphia for many years but not until today do I feel I know it. After visiting Independence Hall, St. Peter's, old Swede's Church, and so many other great landmarks, I feel the whole story of the country and all of the old Colonial part excitingly integrated with a big, vigorous, modern city . . . I walked everywhere . . . it gave me a sense of continuity, reality, and of being a part of America's history, even if I am a New Yorker!"

During the past six or seven years, almost every day, *The Philadelphia Inquirer* and *The Evening Bulletin* have run articles on the city's restoration programs and long-range plans for urban renewal.

There are architectural gems in this "jeweled brooch" which, though they may outwardly appear in good shape, are, at the moment of writing, still undergoing renovations, such as the square brick Free Quaker Meeting House, built in 1783. This Fifth and Arch Street meeting house has been certified as a historic landmark and no longer functions as a place of worship. The Clerk of the Meeting is Reeves Wetherill, public relations executive of the John Wanamaker store. His ancestor, Samuel Wetherill, built the meeting house during the Revolution when the Free (or "Fighting") Quakers — those who participated in one way or another in the war — were read out of the orthodox meetings and needed their own places of worship. Betsy Ross belonged to this meeting.

"Today we have become more of a charity than a religion," says Reeves Wetherill, who, together with other descendants and inheritors of the founders, sold the meeting house to the Commonwealth of Pennsylvania in 1966. There now are plans for inaugurating a permanent series of presentations (through slides of artists' renderings and taped commentaries) on the role Quakers played during the Revolutionary Period, and the building is to be used

21

Opposite: Market Street, looking west.

as a headquarters for the Junior League, which provides the guide service for this district.

Since Quakers believe that women are better equipped to dispense charities than men, forty women out of the members of the Society of Free Quakers divide the yearly accumulated income from the Society's securities, each lady donating a share to a charity of her own choosing. These women must either be birthright members (meaning both father and mother were Quakers) or wives of birthright men.

Shortly after World War II, when Reeves Wetherill returned from serving in the Navy, and before assuming his present position at Wanamaker's, he became Public Relations Director of Gimbels. The dapper, white-haired, and mustachioed president of the store, Ellis Gimbel, asked his new young executive what his religion was. When Reeves replied that he was a Quaker, Mr. Gimbel told him that he had the distinction of being the first Quaker executive ever engaged in this Jewish concern. "And how does it feel to be working with us?" asked Mr. Gimbel.

"The best way I can answer you, sir, is by quoting my family's definition of a Quaker: 'One who buys from a Scotsman, sells to a Jew, and still makes a profit,'" Reeves replied.

From then on, Uncle Ellis (as Gimbels' devoted workers called him) used this story in many a speech — always expecting, and receiving, a gratifying laugh from his audience.

Religious freedom was guaranteed in Pennsylvania by William Penn, but his own faith is still strongly associated with the city, as is the Quaker manner of speech. The quaint custom of addressing one another as "thee" still prevails, although much less than it used to. Mrs. John M. Taylor told me, "I think it has become something like the *tu* in French — very intimate and reserved for family or close friends."

Mrs. Taylor regrets that so few of her Quaker friends now exchange "thees." Nevertheless, Mr. and Mrs. Granville Worrell of Gladwyne, who became Episcopalians, have clung to this Quaker practice.

"I tease them about it," said Mrs. Taylor, "but I also encourage them because I find it such a charming custom and I can't bear to see it go out of style."

It was in the house of one of Mrs. Taylor's ancestors in Spring Hill, Cape Cod, that the first Friends' meeting was held inside four walls in North America. "Before this, of course, persecuted Quakers, rain or shine, congregated for their worship in the open," she explained.

"Perhaps you'd be interested to know that we Quakers perform our own marriage ceremony," Mrs. Taylor said. "When John and I were married, we faced our Elder in the meeting house. First, he said a prayer to us in the presence of our invited guests, who didn't necessarily have to be Friends, in the Quaker sense of the word.

"After a silence, John and I took one another's hands and in turn spoke the following memorized words:'I, John Taylor, take thee, Ellis Phinney, to be my loving faithful wife until death do we separate.' You see, we married ourselves in the presence of God, our Elder, and our friends. After another silence, the Elder spoke a few more words of prayer. It is possible, too, that anyone present, if moved to do so, might have risen and expressed himself or herself. Before leaving the meeting, guests signed their names below that of the bride and groom on a parchment document."

Philadelphia is noted for its numerous Quaker schools, which many Americans consider offer the best all-around education in the country. There are also still a number of active Friends' meeting houses in the region, especially on the Main Line, such as the one on Meeting House Lane, Merion; the one in Villanova, and the one Mrs. Taylor attends, Valley Meeting in the town of King of Prussia.

SHOPS AND RESTAURANTS

Unlike New York, Philadelphia has no café society, smart night clubs, discothèques, or restaurants where reporters go table hopping to pick up gossip for their columns. Publicity, unless connected with something constructive, gets nobody anywhere in Philadelphia.

A glance at the local society column will show that the news is mainly about coming-out parties, weddings, and benefits. It takes resourceful writers — Ruth Seltzer on *The Philadelphia Inquirer* and Joseph X. Dever on *The Evening Bulletin* — to create an illusion of gossip without infringing on people's privacy.

Our most famous living painter, Franklin C. Watkins, has never been tempted to move to New York as have so many American artists from all over the country, because of the sense of privacy he finds at home on Spruce Street. "I like to live in Philadelphia rather than in New York," he says, "because in New York I would feel compelled to keep up with its tempo, whereas in Philadelphia you can see people without their interfering with your work. In New York this might make you feel neglected rather than give you a sense of privacy."

Planting firm roots, fostering family continuity, and living your own private life while helping your community as much as possible is the Philadelphia way of life. Richard Bond, Wanamaker's Chairman of the Board, says, "I go out hardly at all. My philosophy is that while a man or woman can contribute all the time, energy, thought, and enthusiasm he can summon up during the daytime, he or she also owes something to the family."

The Wanamaker store, enormous as it is, nevertheless makes you feel at home; somehow it manages to retain a family feeling, and Strawbridge and Clothier does the same. John Wanamaker, the founder of the famous store, began his career by opening Oak Hall, a men's clothing store, in 1861. He died in 1922, many times a millionaire. Great grandson John R. Wanamaker, who lives with his family in Chestnut Hill, is still Chairman of the Board. If you roam in the store's grand court on the street floor or nestle against the wings of the great eagle statue — Philadelphia's most famous rendezvous spot — it is quite likely that you will run into John Wanamaker.

This sense of family continuity is present in many phases of Philadelphia's industry and business where sons and cousins enter long-established publishing houses, banks, and law firms. Family tradition prevails even in restaurants, such as the *uptown* Bookbinder's on Fifteenth Street, near Locust, an unpretentious but famous sea-food house personally supervised by its solicitous owner, Samuel C. Bookbinder, grandson of the founder. Customers get a kick out of tying bibs around their necks to banquet on steamed clams and lobsters — personally selected from a tank near the entrance.

The original *downtown* 1865 Bookbinder's at Second and Walnut Streets also specializes in sea food, and although the restaurant has been enlarged with faithful attention to tradition by its new owner, John Taxin, it has become a little too sprawling to retain the intimate Bookbinder family touch.

Bob Sigel's restaurant at 1918 Chestnut Street is another old favorite where you are treated with special attention by its handsome sporty owner. The same cordial atmosphere prevails at Bob's sister's restaurant, Helen Sigel Wilson's, on Walnut Street. Though Helen may be more famous as a golf champion, she and her husband are equally successful as restaurateurs.

A lively and overwhelmingly smiling host is Gino, at whose Italian restaurant on Walnut Street you are served with as much singing as spaghetti. Between table hopping, Gino launches into operatic arias, often inspiring customers to join him.

On Sunday nights at Frankie Bradley's on Chancellor Street, a more intimate spot where father, daughter, and son specialize in steaks, you often see theater personalities when stage shows are in town.

"Little Italy," the area around Christian and Ninth Streets, has retained its Sicilian-Neopolitan-Calabrese-Abruzzese ambiance. It is fun shopping there especially on Thursdays and Fridays, when the open stalls are more abundantly filled with fresh fruits, vegetables, sea food, poultry, and meats, and venders shout out their wares and prices — often in native dialect — as you push through the crowded sidewalks. The neighborhood's Corona Di Ferro Restaurant attracts employees of Philadelphia's biggest advertising company, N. W. Ayer, and those members of the Curtis Publishing Company who remained after the bulk of the company's operation moved to New York.

The most fashionable restaurant is in the Barclay Hotel on Rittenhouse Square. Out-of-towners who might be curious about Philadelphia's society should lunch there on a Friday. That day, before an afternoon concert by the Philadelphia Orchestra at the Academy of Music, the Barclay is always monopolized by smartly dressed lady subscribers or members of committees, in from the country. The maître d'hôtel, Mario, has been there long enough to know Philadelphians by name and to remember each one's favorite dish. As for the two "hat-check girls," Christine and Peggy, they have been working in their starched aprons for over thirty-five years. "We can hardly be called hat-check girls," says Christine with a laugh, "we don't have checks — we know everyone by name!"

The Warwick Hotel is also popular, as is the Bellevue-Stratford, possibly more so with out-of-towners than locals.

Philadelphia ladies who find a short, light lunch suits them scoot down to the Walnut Street Colonnade, which they refer to as "The Sunken Ritz," a restaurant run by a chain but meticulously supervised, with plain food served cafeteria-style.

A new Colonnade, also underground, but with a bar, has recently opened in the new Rohm and Haas Building and is filled at noon with people who work in and around Independence Square.

Catering to the residents of the new apartment buildings that have grown up in the center of the city, many new restaurants have opened, such as The Emperor on South Twentieth Street, run by Bob Maxwell, and 1700 down on reclaimed pier No. 37, which commands a splendid view of the Delaware River and the Benjamin Franklin bridge and is especially impressive at night. The best view in town is from the Penthouse Restaurant atop the Lewis Tower at Fifteenth and Locust. Visiting musicians (among them Leonard Bernstein and Van

Cliburn) favor Snockey's on South Eighth Street, with its sea food, tiled walls, and sawdust on the floor. Gourmets seldom seen in restaurants have found a haven in Peter von Starck's new La Panetière on Spruce Street.

Philadelphians agree in general that the best food is served in people's houses, and in the clubs. The Philadelphia Club, one of the oldest and most exclusive men's clubs in the country, the Rittenhouse, the Rabbit, and the Fish House (where the members cook their own specialties), the ladies' eminently respectable Acorn Club, and the Union League's Victorian brownstone on Broad Street, are some that have won reputations for excellent food. One day, while Emlen and I were lunching at the League, our host's eyes twinkled when he told of a gentleman from Kansas City who was put up at the League by one of its members. For two nights in succession the gentleman placed his brown shoes out in the corridor, but nobody polished them. When he inquired about the lack of service, the manager replied simply, "We are sorry, sir, but we don't have brown polish in our club."

One way Philadelphians uphold the reputation of their tables is by doing most of their marketing and cooking themselves. The most famous market — the Reading Terminal under the railroad station at Twelfth and Arch Streets — is a huge area filled with the greatest variety of dairy products, vegetables, fruits, delicacies, and meats that, perhaps, I have ever seen. On the pork counters you find scrapple, which I've always thought was underrated by Philadelphians, even though it is, like pepper pot, one of their native dishes. Every visitor wants to be able to say he has eaten scrapple in Philadelphia. I often serve it at lunch with lentils and salad, which usually makes quite a hit.

Many vegetables are brought in, young and tender, from the Pennsylvania German regions of Lancaster County, some sixty-five miles from Philadelphia. Alas, with a few exceptions, Mennonite farmers coming down as far as the big city have now abandoned their traditional garb — the men, their flat-rimmed black felt hats and bearded faces, and the ladies their bonnets, full long skirts, and fitted bodices. But occasionally you do see one or two — picturesque, and hating to be photographed.

The international air of the Reading Terminal is contributed to by Madame Supiot, who greets one at her long counter, abundantly stacked with verdant salads, chives, parsley, fresh herbs, and flowers, with "Qu'est-ce que vous désirez, Madame?" — and by Dick's Original Place with its fancy breads, cold cuts, and delicacies from Scandinavia, France, Switzerland, Ireland, Poland, and the Baltic States.

At a cool white marble counter you can order Bassett's ice cream, which generations of connoisseurs say is the best in the world. In fact, you can count on good ice cream in Philadelphia just the way you count on the best spaghetti in Italy and fine wines in France.

When Henry Gerstley, president of the Settlement Music School, was president of the Robin Hood Dell concerts, he asked the late Jeanette MacDonald (who was born in Philadelphia) to be a guest soloist and invited her to be guest of honor at a reception afterward. Miss MacDonald's manager answered that the operetta and movie star would be delighted to attend, specifying that she wished no more than twenty people and that she would like chicken sandwiches, white meat only, on white bread with the crusts cut off, and milk and vanilla ice cream. For the other nineteen guests, however, Henry ordered a more elaborate menu. "Miss MacDonald was a delightful guest," he said, "and showed appreciation for the buffet. Later she wrote me thanking me profusely. At the end she added, 'But how *did* you know what I like to eat — especially vanilla ice cream!'"

Visitors who come to Philadelphia to relive its history are usually interested in antiques.

The best street to browse along is Pine, from Ninth to Eighteenth Streets. There are other antique shops farther down, toward Society Hill, their façades remodeled to blend in with the rest of the "old" architecture. But the choicest hang out their shingles between Sixteenth and Seventeenth Streets, where one may find Bullard's, specializing in eighteenth-century English furniture, and Renée Shourdes, who concentrates on china, while Michael Fiorillo, "the Grand Old Man of Pine Street," is in the 1100 block.

Philadelphia is also a center of learning, and has more than an average number of good bookshops for a city its size. Leary's Book Store on Ninth Street below Market is one of the oldest in Philadelphia.

Sessler's Book Store, dating back to 1882, is, of course, a Philadelphia institution. Although the store has moved three times, it has always conveniently remained on Walnut Street, where it maintains an ideal balance between the current output of publishers and rare, out-of-print books. The shop often holds autographing parties for native and visiting authors. Sessler's is presided over from an inner sanctum in the rear by Mabel Zahn, an authority on rare editions and prints, and on autographs and manuscripts as well. Miss Zahn has been with the store all her professional life, since her high school days when she came to help her father, who worked for Charles S. Sessler, the founder. But it was only after Sessler's son Leonard died that Miss Zahn took over.

The personalized shops that so appeal to Philadelphians, from highly selective men's shops and tailors, cheese and other gourmet shops (such as Stuart Lewis's on Locust Street), to boutiques and ladies' apparel shops, are to be found all over town and on the Main Line and Chestnut Hill. The hippies are not forgotten. They can pick up colorful paraphernalia at The Apparatus at 203 South Seventeenth Street.

Some of these shops are run by socialites who serve you personally. Fernanda Wanamaker, one of the first, opened a children's shop called Nana on the Main Line, and the success of this initial venture led to three thriving branches for adults as well as children.

Ann Pakradooni does a brisk business in her Haverford boutique, Joi de Vivre, which features her own custom-designed clothes and accessories.

Mrs. John Hill and Mrs. Michael Cosgrave run the popular Papillon in Bryn Mawr, which was started because "we wanted to get away from mass production, and give our customers the sort of individuality we once yearned to find in clothes for ourselves," Mrs. Cosgrave explained.

In center city, Norma McManus has a tweedy boutique on Sixteenth Street, the Potpourri, where you inch down steps resembling a fire escape, to enjoy hunting through a theatrical display of unusual accessories. Among other successful boutiques are Dorothy Bullitt's in Ardmore, now run by her son, Logan; The Cocked Hat in Wayne; The Pear Tree in Bryn Mawr, run by Betty Van Alen; Tom LaZear's Dress Shop on Locust Street; next door, David Buckner's underground antique nest, Au Bon Gout; and, largest and best known of all, Nan Duskin's on Walnut at Eighteenth — where window mannequins are haughtily posed in creations by top international designers.

Everyone has his or her own favorite village center within the city and in the surrounding suburbs. Not only is there everything everybody needs, but there are many indigenous things that make this city the interesting and lovable place it is to live in.

CREATIVE PEOPLE

Philadelphia is not only rich in what it has to offer in the way of education, medicine, architecture, and sports; it is rich also in its artists, who, whether or not they continue to live here, give the city much devoted support.

Most Philadelphians who marry out of the city or move away for business reasons, such as actors, composers, musicians, and singers, return with affection and are received with the greatest warmth and enthusiasm. Marian Anderson is one of these and another is the great pianist André Watts.

The composer and author Ned Rorem comes home not only to visit his parents but to hear Eugene Ormandy conduct his works with the Philadelphia Orchestra. Samuel Barber, too, is often seen back in town at the Academy of Music, where his symphonies and operas are performed, and he usually drops in on the Efrem Zimbalists' on DeLancey Place. Mrs. Zimbalist, the former Mary Curtis, is the founder of the Curtis Institute of Music on Rittenhouse Square, which was directed by her violinist husband. Whenever I pass by the Institute and hear the sounds of students vocalizing or practicing the piano, I am reminded of how many other former students besides Samuel Barber have become world renowned — Gian Carlo Menotti, for instance.

Gian Carlo's arrival at Curtis was largely due to Toscanini, who convinced Signora Menotti that her son should study with the reknowned teacher Scalero. Mrs. John Braun, board member of the Curtis Institute and a neighbor and friend of Mrs. Zimbalist, told me: "The maestro was teaching at the Curtis and Samuel Barber was studying with him. Gian Carlo came here at the age of sixteen — I'll never forget how homesick he was. The following summer, however, Mary Zimbalist said to me, 'These are two amazing boys, we must do something for them.' She saw to it that they went for the summers to Little Rockport in Camden, Maine. Sam studied conducting and the young Italian composed *Amelia Goes to the Ball*, his first opera.

"Every Christmas since that year they spend with us in DeLancey Place. We're sort of a family — yes, that's the way it is, very sweet and rewarding, but we make it a point not to press them. They come on their own. I just can't believe at times we are in the presence of two geniuses. To us, well, we'll always think of them as little boys." For many years afterward, both composers taught at Curtis as well.

Philadelphia has produced many artists in the field of music — Anna Moffo, the New York Metropolitan Opera soprano, is one. She sings in Philadelphia every season to capacity houses. We gave a small party for her after one of her glorious performances. Her mother and father came with her — they were so proud of their beautiful, dark-haired diva that they barely spoke.

The first time I met Anna Moffo was one evening backstage in the Academy of Music.

Critic Max de Schauensee introduced me to her after her performance as Mimi in *La Bohème.*

"*Bohème* has special significance for me," said Anna. "It was the very first opera I ever heard, right here on this stage. Di Stefano sang Rodolfo and tonight he was scheduled to sing with me — alas, he was ill and couldn't make it.

"It is tremendously thrilling to feel the audience is with you — and tonight I felt it was."

The late Mario Lanza was another of Philadelphia's favorites, and now his mother runs the Mario Lanza Club with the purpose of discovering and fostering young talent.

Also associated with Philadelphia are actors who have become famous on Broadway, in Hollywood, and, in fact, around the world.

The first time I became aware of the fact that the Barrymores came from Philadelphia was when my brother Stiano Braggiotti acted as one of Ethel Barrymore's husbands in *Encore*, which played in Philadelphia at the Walnut Street Theater. "It was fun playing with her in her home town," my brother told me, "because Ethel Barrymore became very nostalgic, especially about her teen-age years when she went to school here. When we passed the Bellevue-Stratford Hotel she would describe to me the elegant balls she attended there and how dressed up she used to be — then sigh, 'Today it is so different. . . .' But," my brother added, "Philadelphia remained her favorite city, and London came next." Stiano also acted with John Barrymore in *My Dear Children*. "John was different — more erratic and not as sentimental about his early days as Ethel was. He was too concerned with the present, and living it up to the hilt."

Few of us can forget the late W. C. Fields, if not in person, then through his comedy roles in films — or perhaps for reportedly having asked that the epitaph on his tombstone read, "Better here than in Philadelphia." Ethel Waters was also born here, and so were Bobby Rydell, Frankie Avalon, Fabian, and Eddie Fisher, who frequently breezes into town for an engagement at the nearby Latin Casino. The list of stars with Philadelphia connections could, of course, fill pages, but I mention only a few more in passing: Gerry Mulligan, Dick Clark, Connie Mack, Joey Bishop, and Martin Gabel, the actor and producer husband of Arlene Francis.

Constantly displaying her affection for Philadelphia is the former Grace Kelly, now Princess Grace of Monaco, who presented her wedding gown to the Fashion Wing of the Philadelphia Museum of Art. In true Philadelphia family style, Princess Grace loves visiting her mother, Mrs. John B. Kelly, her brother Jack, and her sisters, all of whom not only resemble the beautiful ex-movie star but are beauties in their own right. Handsome Jack Kelly is a sculling champion, as was his late father — but that is not all that occupies Jack. As President of the 1976 Bi-Centennial Corporation he is busy making plans with Mr. Henderson Supplee, retired Chairman of the Board of the Atlantic Richfield Company and Chairman of the Bi-Centennial Citizens' Committee, along, of course, with Mayor Tate.

Philadelphia also boasts many writers, who live in or constantly return to the city. Among those who have written about their city is Richard Powell, author of *The Philadelphian*. The late Struthers Burt wrote *Along These Streets*, and his son, Nathaniel Burt, now living in Princeton, wrote the widely read *Perennial Philadelphians*. Barbara Rex's *Vacancy on India Street* also has a local setting. Charles W. Thayer wrote a book about his mother and life on the Main Line, called *Muzzy*. Nicholas L. Wainwright, head of the Philadelphia Historical Society, wrote *Colonial Grandeur in Philadelphia*. Livingston Biddle, Jr., Deputy Chairman of the National Endowment for the Arts, comes every weekend from

Washington to the Main Line with his wife. Among the books he has written, three have a Philadelphia background: *Main Line, Debut,* and *Sam Bentley's Island.*

Other literary stars are native-born Leon Uris, author of *Exodus* and *Battle Cry;* Professor Robert Strausz-Hupé, who wrote, among other books, *The Zone of Indifference* and *In My Time;* Emily Kimbrough (who came to the Main Line after she was married); Clifford Odets; Philadelphia historian E. Digby Baltzell, who lives with his artist wife, Jane Piper, on DeLancey Place; the late Owen Wister, two of whose children still live in his Long House on Bryn Mawr Avenue. The late Christopher Morley used Philadelphia for the locale of *Kitty Foyle,* a best seller of the 1930s. Arthur Lewis, author of *The Day They Shook the Plum Tree,* and children's book authors Marguerite de Angeli and Katherine Milhous also live here. The city and its environs seem to hold a special attraction for writers — there are over two hundred and fifty living in and near Philadelphia.

Catherine Drinker Bowen lives in a cozy house in Bryn Mawr, and her most recent book is *Miracle at Philadelphia.* Betty Fetter, wife of Dr. Ferdinand Fetter, writes under the nom de plume of Hannah Lees; two books of hers which have an unmistakably Philadelphian setting are *Till the Boys Come Home,* about World War II, and *Prescription for Murder.* Jerre Mangione, professor at the University of Pennsylvania, is the author of the best seller *Mount Allegro* and (more recently) *Life Sentences.* Once Emlen and I had the privilege of acting in a tryout dramatization of *Mount Allegro* at the Little Theater on Rittenhouse Street which played to full houses (a seating capacity of fifty!) for its week's run.

Novelist Pearl Buck has said: "Philadelphia has always been a favorite city, ranking in my affections with London and Rome, Peking and Paris. It is a city with an individuality. Put me down there, blindfolded, in the midst of world travel, and I would know where I was. But, like any great city, Philadelphia has smaller cities within itself. It is not all of one piece, and it is never dull."

ART AND
COLLECTORS

In line with the rest of the country, Philadelphia has had its own population and cultural explosion, and each year an increasing number of visitors converge on the city not only to see the historic shrines of America's first capital, but also to hear its famous orchestra and enjoy its art museums.

Music has bloomed perhaps more profusely than the other arts in Philadelphia. We have the Philadelphia Orchestra, Lyric Opera Company, the Philadelphia Grand Opera Company, the Philadelphia Chamber Orchestra Society, Anshel Brusilow's new Chamber Symphony of Philadelphia, the intimate Coffee Concerts at the Philadelphia Civic Center, the All-Star Forum Series, and special musical events presented by the Theater of the Living Arts on South Street. The Philadelphia Chamber Orchestra Society presents concerts by internationally famous ensembles five times a year at the Academy of Music, and the Philadelphia Museum and University Museum also present special concerts. Rudolph Serkin, new director of the Curtis Institute and a long-time Philadelphia resident, is also head of the Marlboro Music Festival in Vermont, and brings a taste of the festival to the city in the Music of Marlboro series. There are the thriving Pennsylvania Ballet Company, the Curtis String Quartet, the delightful Robin Hood Dell summer concerts in East Fairmount Park, and the Summer Festival in Ambler, which was sponsored by Temple University and had its *première* in 1968. The visual arts are very much in evidence at museums and galleries, and Philadelphia is noted for a number of important private collections. The most famous of these, perhaps, is that of the late Dr. Albert C. Barnes, and it is now fortunately open to the public, although visiting hours are not so liberal as those at the Philadelphia Museum of Art (which has a huge general collection of masterpieces), the University Museum (which has archaeological treasures and exhibits of primitive and oriental art), and other institutions.

During Dr. Albert Barnes's eccentric life, many art lovers — in fact most — were denied the privilege of viewing what is one of the world's greatest collections of late-nineteenth- and twentieth-century French paintings. The collection is said to include over a hundred Cézannes and many, many more Renoirs, but the exact figure is not known because the paintings have not yet been completely catalogued. Partly because of his possessiveness and partly because he was snubbed socially, the revengeful "King of Argyrol" would turn people away at the gates, and many bizarre stories are still in circulation about his incredibly insulting remarks to many VIPs. Martha Speiser, who is also a notable collector, once told me, "Albert Barnes was doing his initial buying at the same time as Maurice and I were. Belligerent though he was, it was stimulating to go around with him in Paris. He had a certain ESP for art. There were times, however, when we became afraid to open our mouths. Barnes was fierce and unpredictable, but even if you didn't say anything, he heard you think. There was no getting around the man in a normal, human sort of way.

"In Philadelphia a group of us used to go to the Barneses' house in Merion and listen to Albert lecture about his collection. It was fine until he began to relate pictures to music. He would point to Cézanne's 'Card Players' for instance, and tap ta-ta-ta-Ta, next to the four pipes, in rhythm with the opening bars of Beethoven's Fifth Symphony. It was too much. We stopped going there."

The galleries at the Barnes Foundation in Merion, now run by his secretary of many years, Violette de Mazia, are hung exactly as Dr. Barnes wished them to be, and visitors from all over the world come especially to Philadelphia to see the fabulous collection.

What is encouraging is that so many young couples have started to collect. Defying the well-known hazard — that Philadelphia is too close to New York for comfort — galleries in town and in the suburbs are proving, instead, that there is a most active local market. The Hope and Paul Makler Gallery attracts collectors and so does the Socrates Perakis Gallery; both are on Locust Street. These and Janet Fleisher's Little Gallery on South Seventeenth Street specialize in the work of contemporary artists.

The Art Alliance on Rittenhouse Square, in spite of its old-fashioned atmosphere, reminiscent of the days the Wetherill family lived in the Italian Renaissance mansion (the famous dress designer, Tina Wetherill Leser, was born and brought up there), presents exhibitions of well-established artists as well as young painters and sculptors of merit. Vitrines in the hall display the work of jewelry makers and other local craftsmen.

Although the Art Alliance is a private club, the galleries and special events are open to the public and are free. The dining room and bar are reserved for members and are particularly popular at noon among artists, architects, and city planners. Henry Mitchell, Rafael Sabatini, Theo B. White, Henry Pitz, and Max Arnoff, head of the New School of Music, often lunch there. Max is also a member of the Curtis String Quartet, and is frequently seen at the Art Alliance with other members: Orlando Cole, Jascha Bradsky, and Geoffrey Michaels, or with the Director of the Settlement Music School, Sol Schoenback, and his artist wife, Bertha. Archie, the red-haired bartender, has been at the Alliance so long he knows everyone's first name — and the exact way each member wants his favorite drink concocted.

The Print Club, little more than a block away on Latimer Street, is a quiet serious place devotedly supervised by Bertha Von Moschzisker, who has maintained its international high standard in prints and print-making in the upstairs workshop gallery. Anyone is welcome to come here and browse among the displays and open folders, or sit and enjoy the view of the lovely garden beyond the rear windows.

The Pennsylvania Academy of The Fine Arts is dedicated to the works of American artists, and its annual exhibition of paintings and sculpture, chosen by national juries, also attracts thousands of visitors. The overwhelmingly Victorian building, designed by Frank Furness, has a grand staircase, and rooms with heavy wood paneling and high ceilings. It is the oldest art school and museum in America. The galleries are nevertheless well lit and the annual show, with its coveted prizes, is covered by such critics as *The New York Times*'s John Canaday (who used to live in Philadelphia when he was head of the Education Department of the Philadelphia Museum of Art), Emily Genauer, and other out-of-towners. Most of the teachers at the Academy have national reputations. The best known is Philadelphia's own Franklin C. Watkins, the first living American painter to have been given a one-man show both at the Museum of Modern Art in New York and at the Philadelphia Museum of Art — the last occasion celebrating his seventieth birthday.

Many private Philadelphia collections have so often been described in newspapers and magazines that the owners are always receiving requests from visitors asking if they may see them. Masterpieces from such collections as those of Sturgis Ingersoll, the William Wrights, the Henry Cliffords, Mrs. Herbert C. Morris, Mrs. John Wintersteen, and her brother Henry McIlhenny, have traveled as far as San Francisco, Dallas, and Paris. Probably Philadelphia's most sought-after private collection is that of Henry McIlhenny, which is made up mostly of French paintings of the nineteenth and early twentieth centuries. "I love what I acquire and I love my own parties," says Henry (who incidentally gives some of the best parties in Philadelphia, with some of the best food in the world). "Nothing clicks in life without a sincere sense of enjoyment."

While an undergraduate at Harvard, Henry had already made several major acquisitions, and at twenty-two, inspired by Harvard's professor of art history Dr. Paul J. Sachs, he plunged into his first real buying spree. On the walls of his four-story Victorian mansion on Rittenhouse Square Henry has accumulated such treasures as Toulouse-Lautrec's "Moulin Rouge," Delacroix's "Death of Sardanapalus" (painted after the artist's larger version in the Louvre), an unusual Van Gogh — a blue field streaked with rain — a still life by Matisse, a Cézanne portrait of the artist's wife in a blue and white striped blouse, works by Chardin, David, Renoir, Corot, Seurat, and a pastel study by Degas for his painting "Mary Cassatt au Louvre."

When first exposed to Henry's collection connoisseurs are impressed not only by its carefully selected and well-balanced quality, but by the setting in which the paintings and sculpture come to life. In his often-photographed L-shaped drawing room downstairs he has entertained such guests as Cecil Beaton; Eugene Ormandy; Nicky Mariano; Ambassador and Mme. Hervé Alphand; Loelia, Duchess of Westminster; Noël Coward; Morris Graves; Katherine Drinker Bowen; Tennessee Williams; George Balanchine; and Helen Hayes. Many have stood engulfed in silence before Renoir's "Mlle. LeGrand" hung above an Empire chest, Ingres's "La Comtesse de Tournon" over the nineteenth-century Italian marble mantelpiece with its two green obelisks, or the Degas bronze of a ballerina near one of the garden windows.

Today Henry's sister, Mrs. John Wintersteen, who lives in Villanova, has become equally well known for her active participation in the world of art. As the first woman president of the Philadelphia Museum of Art she instigated many timely, popular, and vital events, bringing to the museum a much larger number of visitors than ever before. With her unbounded energy and radiant personality, Bonnie inspired people not only to join committees but to give more for the museum's support, and donations have increased fivefold since she became president. Bonnie's stature as a civic leader was climaxed in January 1967, when she received the Gimbel Award for "tireless dedication to the civic and cultural life of Philadelphia and her great influence in the world of art."

Both Bonnie and Henry seem to have inherited a lasting interest in and attachment to the museum from their father, John D. McIlhenny, who was its president from 1918 until he died in 1925.

"It was through our father that we, as children, met many museum directors all over Europe and such great men in the world of art as Richard Offner and Bernard Berenson. I guess we were naturally born museum people," Bonnie says. In fact, Henry McIlhenny held the post of Curator of Decorative Arts for thirty years before retiring in 1964, the year before his sister became president.

Though Bonnie Wintersteen's collection includes such important works as Matisse's "Woman in Blue" and Brancusi's statue "Mademoiselle Pogany," her collection is best known for its Picassos. "If I notice a Picasso in any exhibition I am drawn to it as if by a magnet," she says. "I believe he is the greatest art power the world has ever had."

In the life of a curator of painting, the drive for collecting pictures often carries over into his own house. This is certainly true of Henry Clifford, who was Curator of Paintings at the Philadelphia Museum of Art for over thirty years. When he and his wife Esther are not in their Villa Capponi in Florence, or in their vast chalet on Mont Pèlerin-sur-Vevey in Switzerland or their house in Mexico, they live in their Italian-style mansion at Radnor, where their main collection is housed. Their large drawing room is radiant with light, flowers, and pictures ranging from the well-known "Storm in the Jungle" by le Douanier Rousseau to the works of Paul Klee, Eugène Berman, Tchelichev, Miró, and Picasso. Henry and Esther are also ballet enthusiasts, and I remember well the amusing pre-World War II parties they gave in honor of various visiting ballet companies. Lichine, Riabouchinska, Danilova, Frederic Franklin, Toumanova, Baronova, Eglevsky, Uskevitch, Sono Osato, and many more would troop out to the country on a Sunday to enjoy the Cliffords' warm hospitality.

The Rodolphe de Schauensees also have a notable art collection in their large house in Devon, where they live with one of their twin daughters, Maude, an archaeologist, and their sprightly Bouvier de Flandres dogs. The de Schauensees believe in mixing what is recognized as great with what might possibly become so, and with what just happens to appeal to them anyway. The walls of their drawing room are hung with Van Gogh's "Boy with Béret," a Renoir nude, a Degas dancer, and a Gauguin landscape, among other masterpieces. Besides these they treasure their collection of pictures by contemporary Philadelphians such as Franklin Watkins, Hobson Pittman, Walter Stuempfig, and others.

Rudy de Schauensee, an ornithologist, and Vice-President of the Academy of Natural Sciences, has written books about his specialty — South American birds. Many specimens collected during his travels to South America are displayed in large vitrines in one of the many interesting rare-animal exhibits to be seen at the Academy.

Another of Philadelphia's eminent art collectors — and civic leaders — is Mrs. Herbert C. Morris. Aside from having given the gold and white ballroom to the Academy of Music in memory of her late husband, "Billie" Morris not only is on the board of the Philadelphia Museum of Art, but is also on the boards of the Lyric Opera Company, the Philadelphia Orchestra, the America-Italy Society, and other organizations. As if this were not enough, Billie's parties at her house in Bryn Mawr usually had art or music as a central theme. The drawing room, with its vine-covered wall and swimming pool, was a delightful setting for these events. During an evening at Billie's, you might well be entertained by the Curtis Quartet, or meet Picasso's friend Françoise Gilot and see an exhibition of her paintings in her new house in Society Hill.

Though collectors live their normal lives with characteristic Philadelphia reserve, they nevertheless feel a responsibility to share their beautiful paintings and sculpture with as many people as possible. This is certainly true of the Malcolm Eisenbergs, who live on DeLancey Place Malcolm is on the board of the Theatre of the Living Arts, and has often entertained such strong believers and supporters as Mrs. Nancy Grace, Mr. and Mrs. Douglas Lovell, Miss Ann Stokes, Mr. and Mrs. Peter Godfrey, as well as many of the Theatre's creative people. I am thinking in particular of Frank Weiss, the ingenious architect who transformed a derelict movie house into the off-Broadwayish Theatre of the Living Arts, with its "modular" stage, and beloved Samuel Rosenbaum, the Theatre's founder and former chairman of the board.

Much credit rightly goes to young collectors who believe in what they like, who watch values in the art market jump up and down as fast as a pogo stick, and who then buy at the right moment. What is "in" today may be "out" tomorrow, and the wise collector, in buying what he likes at a price he can afford, enjoys his collection regardless of its ultimate value.

A good example of the avant-gardiste with no ulterior investment motives, acting entirely on personal taste, is Mrs. H. Gates Lloyd, whose Philadelphia upbringing was conservative. In the late thirties and forties, operating on a small budget, Lallie barged into the world of abstract art. She bought only what she liked and ignored the "my own child could do better than that" remarks of many of her friends. Today, however, not many children are considered to have done better than Pollock, Rothko, Kline, Motherwell, Calder, Moore, Burri, and the many other artists represented in the Lloyd collection.

A lively new generation of Philadelphia collectors is following in the Lloyds' footsteps. New ideas have cracked Philadelphia's rigid spine, and collectors with open minds and unusual interests are supporting modern art as never before.

An avid gallery-goer, Mrs. Josiah Marvel is one who prefers twentieth-century art and courageously buys work of promising young students. Many of them are frequent guests at her house, which is alive with famous local artists such as Andrew Wyeth.

The Jack Wolgins and architect Marechal Brown have concentrated on the Surrealist period, believing that it has not as yet come to its apex of appreciation. A sunburst by Bertoia beams in the Wolgins' white apartment amid some splendid di Chiricos, Magrittes, and unique Marcoussis. The Richard Kaplans and the N. Richard Millers complement primitive art with contemporary works.

In the DeLancey Place house of the Meyer Potamkins a superb representation of the Ash Can School of painting is mixed with primitive art and English furniture. Three blocks away on DeLancey Place, in the home of the Benjamin D. Bernsteins, an astonishing variety of paintings hangs practically from floor to ceiling in the house.

Philadelphia is also lucky to have a rising generation of up-and-coming collectors from the Main Line, such as the John T. Dorrances, the William P. Woods, the David Pincuses, who are champions of Pop Art in Philadelphia, and the Paul M. Ingersolls, who not only are collectors but also work hard to bring new blood to the Philadelphia Museum of Art.

The William Wolgins are almost as famous for their private penthouse pool atop the Drake Hotel and the dizzy film sequences Andy Warhol made there as they are for their collection.

Henry Gardiner, Assistant Curator of Paintings at the Philadelphia Museum of Art, says, "In the past ten years Philadelphia's artistic life has accelerated into a most meritorious period of progress and probing into all new forms of creativeness. Philadelphia collectors, free from commercial pressures and overcloseness to New York's monumental output of art, can come home, after being exposed to New York's galleries and museums, and are able to take time to get a perspective and more easily make astute selections."

Certainly, since the resurgence of town living, Philadelphia can hardly any longer be called a "sleepy town." Recently Samuel A. Green, the former Director of the Institute of Contemporary Art at the University of Pennsylvania, imported the explosive Andy Warhol show that crammed over seven thousand people into the Institute's three galleries. The unruly crowd was more anxious to see Andy and his entourage than his art, so the paintings had to be taken down. For the rest of the opening, the walls were empty. "But nobody cared," said Sam, shrugging his shoulders. "They saw what they wanted: Warhol in the flesh."

Local art news hit out-of-town newspapers and the national magazines again when the MOM (Museum of Merchandise) show at the Arts Council of the YMHA opened. This pioneering group presented a way-out exhibition and fashion show in a dizzy atmosphere of shimmering lights, smoke, and noise. In spite of its sometimes outrageous contents the show may well have planted useful seeds of creativeness for future consumer goods. The idea for the show was conceived by Joan Kron and Audrey Sabol, who gathered together disparate items including Andy Warhol's creation of a new cologne called "You're In" packaged in a silver Coca-Cola bottle, a boat with a sail hand-painted by Larry Zox, a clock with "familiar hands" by Robert Filliou, moving "haikus" by Bici Hendricks, projected on a wall from a tape-fed machine, and "edible art" by Les Levine, dispensed by a vending machine. Said Joan Kron of the latter, "When you are fed up with this art, you can eat it." Mrs. Sabol wore a brooch with a dinerlike neon sign with the word EAT blinking on it. But don't let Mrs. Samuel Kron or Mrs. Edwin Sabol's odd productions or remarks throw you off. Both ladies and their husbands belong to a group of serious and vital collectors who have helped the Institute of Contemporary Art become a beacon of avant-gardism in Philadelphia. Many more such foresighted art lovers whose collections were once sneered at are now pounced upon to lend their pictures, sculptures, and constructions to current exhibitions.

Some of these are among the six hundred or more members of the "Friends of the Philadelphia Museum of Art," who encourage greater enthusiasm in the museum's activities, develop vital and varied programs, and donate works of art to the museum.

"That many members of a group so oriented to extending the Museum's collections should be private collectors is hardly surprising," says Evan H. Turner, the Museum's director. "The Friends have, therefore, devised the idea of stimulating more collections in the community by organizing this selection of works borrowed from their membership. The range of material is as varied as might be expected, but the variety of taste is particularly startling. The Museum may proudly be confident of its future when its community can produce so many discriminating collectors."

A liking for good food often seems to go hand in hand with a taste for beautiful pictures. It is true in the case of Henry McIlhenny's household; it is also true at Inwood, the Wynnewood home of Walter H. Annenberg, publisher of *The Philadelphia Inquirer*. The Annenbergs' swimming pool and nine-hole golf course offer plenty of exercise before a gourmet dinner and the pleasures of conversation.

While the Annenbergs' art collection does include the works of American artists, including an important Andrew Wyeth, their passion is for nineteenth-century French painting. Many are displayed in the large drawing room with the Adam furniture, and look extraordinarily well against antique Chinese wallpaper.

One sometimes wonders if any other city in the world can boast as many Renoirs, Gauguins, and Cézannes as there are in Philadelphia collections.

The Annenbergs' most recent acquisition is Renoir's "Daughter of Catulle Mendès." They own two Gauguins as well as a Cézanne, "Mont Ste. Victoire," a Degas, "Modiste," and Van Gogh's "Les Oliviers," to mention some of their treasures.

The Annenbergs are also noted for their interest in American history. They own a Gilbert Stuart portrait of George Washington, and during the Kennedy Administration they donated to the White House the well-known "thumb portrait" of Benjamin Franklin by William Alexander. They are "angels" of the Hill-Keith Physick House, a Society Hill landmark restored by George B. Roberts and decorated by George Doan. Mr. Annenberg is a trustee of the University of Pennsylvania, which is closely associated in history with his great idol, Benjamin Franklin.

There are not many private collections in Philadelphia which specialize in outdoor sculpture. Best known is that of R. Sturgis Ingersoll, former president of the Philadelphia Museum of Art and a partner of the law firm of Ballard, Spahr, Andrews and Ingersoll. Tall and lanky, Sturgis is always visible in a crowd. In spite of his old-fashioned twirled mustache, he is and has always been ahead of the crowd when it comes to sculpture or paintings. It is often said that it was he who introduced Picasso to Philadelphia.

Sturgis has created a lovely and exciting three-acre sculpture garden at his place in Pennlyn. A Maillol life-size nude, Picasso's "Man with a Goat," works by the American sculptor Flanagan, and about thirty other important pieces appear comfortably at home among shrubs, trees, and lawn. Friends and art connoisseurs congregate in the garden for Sunday lunch and, after a stroll admiring the sculpture, move indoors. Paintings fill every available wall space, sometimes in odd juxtaposition, arranged at random above sofas, desks, and tables. Picasso's "Calf Bearer" and African bronze sculptures from the kingdom of Benin gaze up at paintings by Matisse, di Chirico, Modigliani, Courbet, and Degas.

An entire book could be written about Philadelphia's collectors and native artists. Philadelphia, so often described as the Quaker City or City of Brotherly Love, could certainly be also called the City of Collectors.

Benjamin Franklin Parkway and City Hall from the steps of the Philadelphia Museum of Art. *Overleaf*: North Broad Street.

Newsstand at Thirteenth and Market.

Winter evening in Chestnut Street.

Homebound Mainliners on the Paoli Local.

Workmen on a downtown building.

Right: The Municipal Services Building.

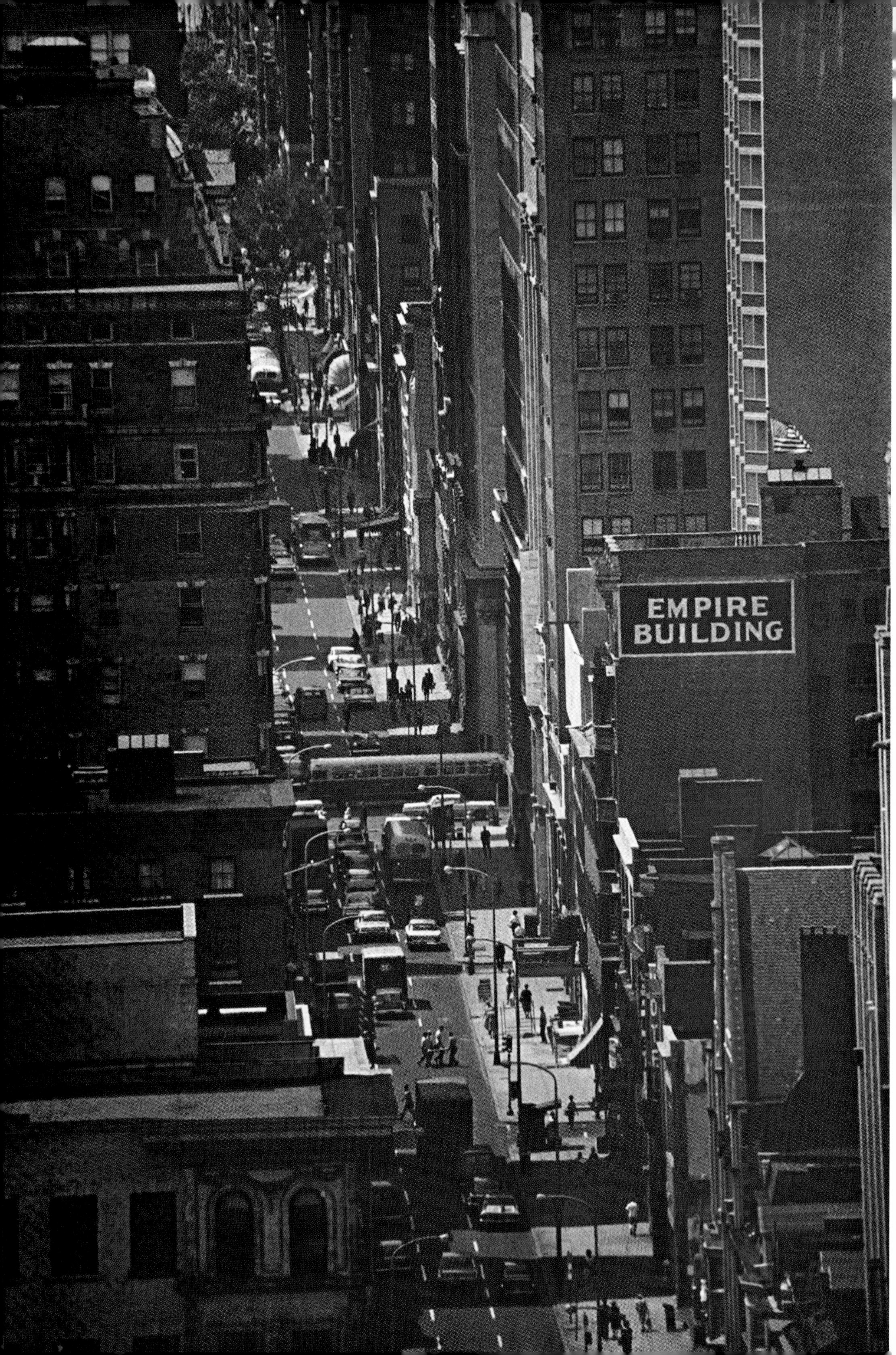
EMPIRE
BUILDING

Left: Midafternoon on Walnut Street. *Above:* City Hall tower seen through the flags of the Convention and Visitors' Bureau.

Below: Street signs at the center of the city.

Overleaf: The morning rush at Broad and Chestnut Streets (*left*), and (*right*) scenes along Market Street.

Above: Reflections in the window of the Hospitality Center.

Left: Bus emerging from the lower level at Penn Center.

Right: The new Stock Exchange Building.

Overleaf: Broad and Vine Streets, through a rain-drenched window.

Christmas fantasy in Wanamaker's Grand Court
(*left and above*) and along Chestnut Street (*right*).

Overleaf and following pages: The annual Mummers' Parade.

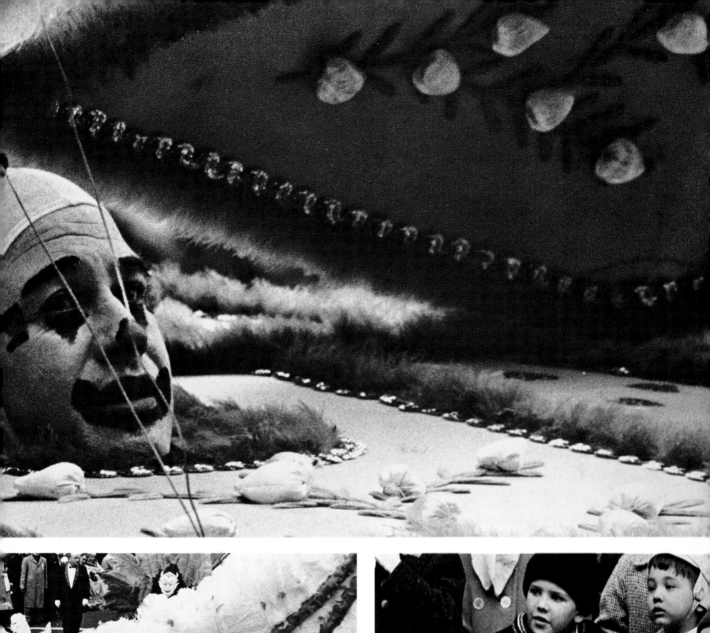

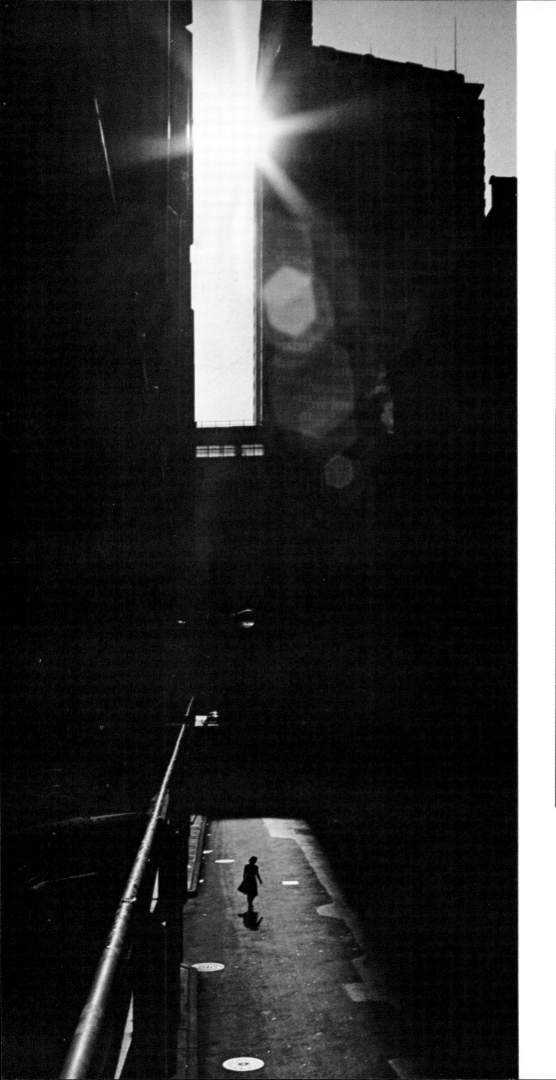

Evening falls on Fairmount Park and the city.

Left: The sun struggles to light the dim canyons near Tenth and Chestnut Streets.

Above and right: Thirtieth Street Station of the Penn Central.

Overleaf: The city at night, looking west from City Hall Tower.

Mrs. Henry Meigs, with a portrait done by her great aunt, Mary Cassatt.

R. Sturgis Ingersoll.

Mr. John R. Wanamaker.

Howard Peterson, President of the Fidelity Bank.

Mrs. Walter H. Annenberg.

Mrs. Joseph Fox Tilghman.

Joseph T. Fraser, Jr., Dean of the Pennsylvania Academy of the Fine Arts.

Rodolphe M. de Schauensee.

Left: Clothesline Art Exhibit in Rittenhouse Square.

Right: The Barclay Hotel, with its fashionable restaurant, is a popular gathering place.

Below: Friends are often encountered in the Square.

Overleaf: Albert Laessle's famous bronze goat in snow-covered Rittenhouse Square.

The open squares of Penn's "greene countrie towne"
are the favorite gathering places of young and old.

Overleaf: The house of art collector Henry P. McIlhenny in Rittenhouse Square.

Henry P. McIlhenny's long hall leading into his L-shaped drawing room. At
the end of the room is Jacques-Louis David's painting of Pope Pius VII and
Cardinal Ceprara. On the left hangs Degas' "Le Viol," and on the right is one
of Delacroix's versions of the "Death of Sardanapalus."

Below: Ingres' portrait of "La Comtesse de Tournon" hangs above the early nineteenth-century Italian mantlepiece in the drawing room. Other paintings in the room are Lautrec's "Moulin Rouge," Degas' "La Danse," "Mademoiselle Le Grand" by Renoir, and "Rain" by Van Gogh.

DeLancey Place.

St. James Place.

Above and left: The Victorian drawing room in the DeLancey Place house of Mr. and Mrs. George Brooke Roberts. The portrait of Mr. Roberts and his daughter Alice is by Walter Stuempfig.

Overleaf: Gingko trees and colored façades of Panama Street.

Eugene Ormandy rehearses the Philadelphia Orchestra.

Interior of the Academy of Music. *Above*: Anna Moffo during a performance.

Above: The brilliantly lighted Academy of Music extends a glowing welcome as the audience arrives for an anniversary concert.

Left: In the gold and white ballroom of the Academy of Music, Mrs. Stuart F. Louchheim greets Mr. and Mrs. Elias B. Wolfe in the receiving line at the dinner which preceded the concert. *Center:* Stuart F. Louchheim, president of the Academy, reviews the program with Mrs. John Wintersteen. *Right:* Mrs. Louchheim with Stuart T. Saunders, chairman of the board of the Penn-Central Railroad, and Mrs. Saunders.

Overleaf: Debutante balls at the Bellevue-Stratford form an important part of the Philadelphia social season.

Below: Mrs. Alexander Biddle and Mrs. Herbert C. Morris find time for a chat before the dinner *(left)*, and *(right)* Mrs. H. Gates Lloyd and Alexander Biddle study the elaborate menu.

Right: Getting commencement snapshots.

Below: The gates of Temple University.

Far right: Strollers on the University of Pennsylvania campus.

Overleaf: Dormitory quadrangle at the University of Pennsylvania.

Left and below: Imaginative playgrounds offer pleasure to the young.

Logan Circle and the Parkway and (*at left*) the Cathedral of Sts. Peter and Paul.

Overleaf: Students at work in the Pennsylvania Academy of the Fine Arts.

The Calder fountain in Logan Square.   *Right:* Statue of Benjamin Franklin in the Franklin Institute.

Left: Children inspect a World War II fighter plane at the Franklin Institute. *Above*: Absorbed audience at a Philadelphia Museum of Art lecture. *Below*: Hadrosaurus dinosaur in the Academy of Natural Sciences. *Overleaf*: In the Rodin Museum. The sculptor's "The Kiss" is at left.

Above and right: Children playing in the fountain pools below the columns of the Philadelphia Museum of Art

Preceding pages: Priest deity from Piedras Negras (*left*), and (*right*) fetish figure from the Lower Congo, both in the University Museum.

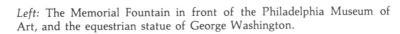

Left: The Memorial Fountain in front of the Philadelphia Museum of Art, and the equestrian statue of George Washington.

Below, left: "Prometheus," by Jacques Lipschitz.

Below: Sculptures by Jacob Epstein, outside the Museum.

Overleaf: The Philadelphia Museum of Art from the Benjamin Franklin Parkway.

Fireworks, balloons, and illumination are part
of the Arts Festival scene at the Museum.

Opposite: Museum pedestals and terraces form a popular playground. *Opposite, below:* Romance on the banks of the Schuylkill. *Below:* Children play along the river bank.

Sculptures in the Ellen Phillips Samuel Memorial on the East River Drive.

The University of Pennsylvania varsity crew goes out for practice.

Overleaf: Boathouses along the Schuylkill. The sculling here, immortalized in Thomas Eakins' paintings, draws thousands for the international regattas.

Fairmount Park and the city skyline, from the Belmont Mansion.

The quiet Schuylkill winds through the park.

Overleaf: One of the historic houses in Fairmount Park, Mount Pleasant, seen through a gazebo.

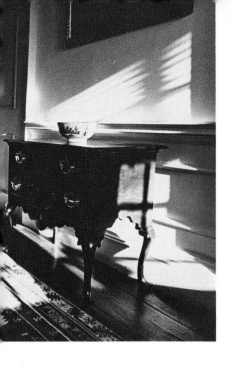

The Philadelphia Museum of Art has filled Mount Pleasant
with paintings and furnishings appropriate to its period.

Animals in the Philadelphia Zoological Garden, the oldest zoo in America.

Left: The exhibits and the spectators take a friendly interest in one another.

Below: Impala fountain at the zoo, designed by Philadelphia sculptor Henry Mitchell.

Overleaf: The Police Administration Building at Seventh and Race Streets, designed by Geddes, Brecher, Qualls, and Cunningham.

Preceding pages: The Bell Telephone Company of Pennsylvania headquarters at One The Parkway, the work of Maurice Fletcher (*left*), and (*right*) Temple Beth Sholom, designed by Frank Lloyd Wright, in Elkins Park.

Above and left: Louis I. Kahn's famous Richardson Towers.

Overleaf: Reading rooms of the business branch of the Free Library *(left),* and *(right)* Walnut Street shoppers.

Efrem Zimbalist, Director Emeritus of the Curtis Institute.

Anna Moffo with impresario Aurelio Fabiani of the Philadelphia Lyric Opera Company, in her dressing room at the Academy of Music.

Mr. and Mrs. John B. Kelly, Jr.

Attorney Frank M. Truscott.

Emerson Greenway, director of the
Philadelphia public library system.

Edmund N. Bacon, Executive Director of
the Philadelphia City Planning Commission.

Mrs. Cummins Catherwood.

Leopold Stokowski with television personality Marciarose.

Overleaf: Playgoers gather at the Walnut Street Theater.

Evan Turner, Director of the
Philadelphia Museum of Art.

Franklin Watkins,
famous Philadelphia paint

Dr. I. S. Ravdin, former Vice-President for Medical Affairs at the University of Pennsylvania Hospital.

Mrs. George M. Cheston, celebrated Philadelphia hostess.

Lawrence Le Page, Chairman
of the Board of the Franklin Institute.

Nicholas B. Wainwright, head of the
Historical Society of Pennsylvania.

Mrs. Reeves Wetherill at her DeLancey Place house.

Marian Anderson.

Left: Statue of banker Robert Morris, Revolutionary War financier, faces the Greek Revival façade of the Second Bank of the United States, built in 1824 and now a museum.

Independence Hall.

Above and right: The Liberty Bell hangs in the stairwell of Independence Hall.

Overleaf: Independence Hall, from Fifth Street.

PASS AND St
PHILADA
MDCCLII

Interior of Christ Church.

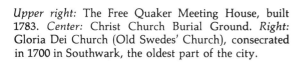

Upper right: The Free Quaker Meeting House, built 1783. *Center:* Christ Church Burial Ground. *Right:* Gloria Dei Church (Old Swedes' Church), consecrated in 1700 in Southwark, the oldest part of the city.

Operating theater and stairwell of the Pennsylvania Hospital.

Left: The modest grave of Benjamin Franklin and his wife Deborah in Christ Church cemetery. *Above:* Carpenter's Hall on Chestnut Street, meeting place of the first Continental Congress.

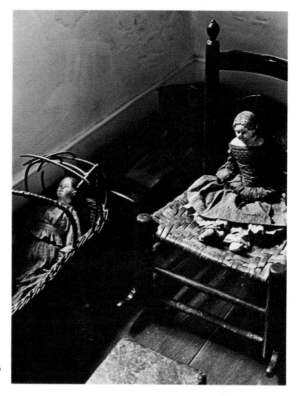

Left: Elfreth's Alley, off Second Street near Arch Street. The houses, dating *c.* 1700, are still occupied.

Right and below: Birthplace of the Stars and Stripes: two interior views of the Betsy Ross House at 239 Arch Street.

Curtis Publishing Company on Washington Square, center of Philadelphia's publishing industry.

Interior of Philosophical Hall on Independence Square, home of the American Philosophical Society.

Above: Cobbled street next to Philosophical Hall. *Left:* Newsboy crosses Market Street with the evening papers. *Below:* Leary's Book Store on South Ninth Street. *Overleaf:* Walt Whitman Bridge and the city, late afternoon in summer.

The Frankford El leaves the Fifteenth and Market Streets station (*above*) and (*below*) takes a sharp curve near Front and Market Streets.

Left: Admiral Dewey's flagship, the *Olympia*, docked below the Benjamin Franklin Bridge.

Ship passing beneath the Walt Whitman Bridge.

The Benjamin Franklin Bridge.

The Philadelphia Eagles at Franklin Field.

Overleaf: The Penn Relays, highlight of the spring season for high school and college hopefuls.

Above: Fans cheer the Phillies at Connie Mack Stadium. *Left:* Gene Mauch, manager of the Philadelphia baseball team. *Right:* Tense moments in the game.

Historic Society Hill is rapidly being restored to its former dignity as a fashionable residential district. *Right:* The old houses of Fifth Street, looking east toward the Delaware River.

Overleaf: Locust Street, near Fifth, was one of the first rejuvenated areas.

Restorations at Second and Spruce Streets.

The Old Philadelphia Development Corp. has saved many fine old buildings from destruction.

Modern town houses off Washington Square.

Above: The clock and cupola of Head House, built in 1805 at the head of the old Second Street Market. *Left:* Smart shops and restaurants now occupy the restored buildings in the area.

Iron railings and cobbled pavements
are characteristic of old Philadelphia.

Head House.

The shade of young trees dapples the old façades of Locust Street.

Society Hill Towers, apartment complex designed by I. M. Pei, soars
above a four-acre plaza decorated with bronze statues by Leonard Baskin.

A class meets outdoors at Bryn Mawr College.

The Administration Building.

The college library.

Haverford, a Quaker college in the Main Line
suburbs, retains an air of academic serenity.

The college observat

Main Line homes are masked by shrubbery.

The Merion Cricket Club in Haverford.

Lynnewood Hall in Elkins Park, once the estate of Peter A. B. Widener, and now a convent.

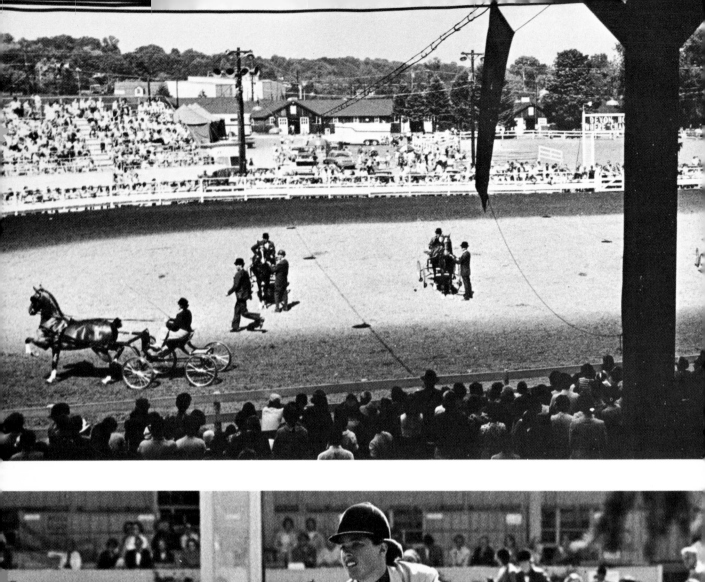

Scenes at the Devon Horse Show, held every year in June.

Whitemarsh Hall, the old Stotesbury Mansion.

"THE COUNTRY"

Millions of Americans associate Philadelphia's Main Line with a famous school or college — Baldwin, Bryn Mawr, Episcopal Academy, the Friends Central School, Haverford, Shipley, or Villanova, to name a few. To many Philadelphians, the older ones especially, the Main Line still means "the country"; to younger ones it may simply mean Philadelphia, for the city has extended so far out, eating into the vast "country estates," that the dividing line is almost impossible to establish.

The quickest route to Haverford, Ardmore, Radnor, Devon, Newtown Square, or any of the Main Line communities is the new Schuylkill Expressway; the most picturesque way is along the West River Drive, with its pleasant view of boathouses and clubs. Coming home at night it is worth taking the drive merely to see the Philadelphia Museum illuminated in a glory of golden light. Or you may join the commuters on the train, and take the unique Paoli local with its toylike whistle, so familiar to all Main Liners.

My associations with the Main Line began in Haverford, where we lived during our first years of marriage. I still love to visit the rural back roads winding past beautifully kept estates, lawns, picket fences, rock gardens, creeks, woods, and fieldstone houses, half hidden by trees and shrubs.

Across College Avenue from where we lived, the gray stone buildings of Haverford College and the landscaping of the campus reminded me of England. In the grounds, a "nature path" winds past a brook which looks most inviting in spring, surrounded by ferns, jack-in-the-pulpits, and crocuses. Of particular interest to horticulturalists are the three hundred or more rare trees, all identified by labels. The most famous tree is an ancient elm, the only living offshoot of the tree under which William Penn signed the treaty with the Indians. In 1835, this Quaker college commissioned an Englishman, William Carville, to landscape its arboretum, which is kept unpublicized in order to avoid attracting sightseers who might disturb the academic serenity. It took some ten years to complete the planting. During this time Carville introduced cricket to the College, and the game is still played against Harvard and other college teams. Cricket is associated more with Philadelphia than with any other American city, and many clubs are still called "cricket clubs." The Merion Cricket Club in Haverford is host to national and international tennis matches.

The beauty of the Main Line counties (once away from the expressways, pikes, main streets, and shopping centers) has attracted many artists. Gimbel Award winner Virginia McCall paints her poetic still lifes and garden scenes as quietly and diligently as a nun; Hobson Pittman, who lives on Bryn Mawr's Old Gulph Road, paints eerie half-real, half-dreamlike interiors and gardens. Hobson's studio overlooks his garden and faces the grounds of the beautiful Church of the Redeemer, a fashionable landmark of the area.

The Main Line continues to attract — and retain — the descendants of Philadelphia families who made this region as well as that of Chestnut Hill and Germantown, across the Schuylkill, among the best-kept suburbs in the world, with dwellings ranging in size from modest-sized houses to palaces modeled after Hampton Court, the Pavillon de la Lanterne, and Versailles.

The broad span of the suburbs and the erratic roads between towns perhaps are reasons why Philadelphians limit their social circles. More likely, though, Main Liners entertain in intimate and carefully selected groups because of family connections and childhood friendships. It seems that almost all of our best friends on the Main Line went to more or less the same schools, have fathers who belonged to the same clubs, and have assembled at the same gatherings since childhood. Contrary to New Yorkers, who brighten up at the meeting of a celebrity or "new face," Philadelphians prefer privacy to publicity and repetition to novelty.

When I first arrived in Philadelphia, many people commiserated hypocritically: "You poor thing, coming from New York to this stick-in-the-mud town." I soon learned that denigrating their town to outsiders was merely their way of fortifying the walls around their inner circles, protecting themselves from "foreign" invasion. Philadelphians seem to feel they have inherited the privilege of tearing down their city, but that no newcomer may practice this "sport" — if he does, he may never get a chance to do so again.

Sean O'Faolain said of Philadelphia, "It is a city never fully satisfied with itself but always fond of itself; occasionally silent, gazing at itself, spellbound, more often ready to talk about itself, uttering all those private little jokes and family passwords that turn every family into a secret society and make every newcomer feel an outsider." But if you show no signs of inferiority at being treated as an outsider and preserve your own identity as a "foreigner" rather than strive to be "one of them," by, for instance, adopting the liberty of running down their city, you may, at long last, be "accepted" — especially, of course, if you marry a Philadelphian!

Philadelphians are often compared to Bostonians because of similarities in their historical backgrounds, intellectual tastes, and snobbery. But Philadelphians are not as cold or austere as their northern cousins. They have been fanned by warm breezes blowing from Baltimore and Charleston, from which cities many families have stemmed. They exude a friendly warmth, extend a generous hospitality, and maintain a disarming sense of humor about themselves.

Philadelphia maintains a strong hold on its children. Now and then the young ones, feeling cramped by a certain stodginess, flee to the freedom of a more anonymous and sparkling life in New York; but it is usually difficult to make a complete break. Mrs. Edwin Fish of New York, formerly Rosemary Howe of Philadelphia, was consulted by a débutante anxious to escape from "dull Philadelphia." "My dear," said Rosie, "the only means of getting out of Philadelphia is to marry out as I did. It's the only sure way." For me, it was the opposite. I married a Philadelphian as the surest way of never getting out.

A Texan married to a young Philadelphia socialite once remarked to a famous hostess, "What a great privilege it must be for you to be a descendant of William Penn." "Oh, dear, yes," said she, "but good heavens! — we've descended so far . . . "

Philadelphians have not descended so very far. While gracefully accepting the inroads of progress which have transformed the quaint Colonial capital of the fledgling United States into a roaring modern city of over two million inhabitants, they have clung tenaciously to customs and manners which have preserved in Philadelphia a gracious way of life found in few other American cities, in fact, probably in no other city.

The defenders of this way of life are the established families of Philadelphia. Every metropolis has its family names which echo its history, culture, and society. Rome has its Borgheses, Viscontis, and Pallavicinos; Paris, its Polignacs; and Philadelphia its Biddles, Cadwaladers, Ingersolls, Roberts, Wisters, and others. The mere mention of one of these families to a Philadelphian evokes a sense of security, of continuity of power, position, and civic leadership.

There are still descendants of old Philadelphia families who live in the same houses they and their families were born and brought up in; who still follow their grandfathers' or great-grandfathers' businesses and cherish the traditions of an earlier day. If they may sometimes appear overly self-satisfied it is but a facade to shield themselves against the insistent intrusions of the modern world, which tend to dilute rather than solidify family steadfastness. It is true that most families who have owned vast acreages have been driven by mounting taxes to break them up. Nevertheless, whenever possible, the family retains a respectable portion in order to live in the ancestral *terra natale*.

Most Philadelphia families bought land in already established Chestnut Hill and Germantown as well as the newer Main Line during the 1870s and the 1880s, when the Pennsylvania Railroad established suburban service on twenty miles of its main route to the west. The railroad stimulated settlement by building a string of resort hotels (what is now Baldwin School in Bryn Mawr was one of them) and by insisting that top railroad executives support the trend by establishing large estates there.

Today, much of it is hardly recognizable. Since World War II, estates have been split up and leveled to make lots for ranch-style houses in place of the stately trees which once graced these undulating hills. Day-to-day living has been simplified by the mushrooming of shopping centers, department stores, and speedways with convenient exits which cater to the interests of expanding population. Suburban towns, once widely separated, each with recognizable characteristics, are now connected and unified by an almost continuous chain of modern "centers," all looking more and more alike.

Yet bastions of that distant age remain and some Philadelphians blindfold themselves to rapidly changing times, clinging to their beloved Main Line, and to as many traditional associations and events as possible. The famous Radnor Hunt, the Gulph Mills Club, the Bryn Mawr Horse Show, the Devon Horse Show, and the national tennis matches at the Merion Cricket Club have an undimmed attraction.

The most exclusive gathering of all is the Assembly Ball at the Bellevue-Stratford at Christmas time. This historic ball maintains traditions unbroken for two centuries. In New York, divorced couples may be snatched out of the Social Register, but remarried divorcées in Philadelphia face a more "serious" consequence. They are dropped from the Assembly, and when they fall from such heights, their social bruises are painful. Moreover, what it takes to be invited to the Assembly Ball is more than family background and financial substance. The late multimillionaire Joseph Widener, even though married to socialite Ella Pancoast, was rejected. The "managers" simply did not care for him. As a result his fabulous art collection, containing some of the best El Grecos in existence, went to the National Gallery of Art in Washington rather than being preserved in Philadelphia.

A male descendant of a member of the Assembly is automatically invited to the Ball, while a woman can be dropped from the list if she marries a nonmember. Ever since the Bellevue-Stratford Hotel was built in 1904 the Ball has been held there, and Meyer Davis and his orchestra are as much a part of this white-tie-and-tails affair as is the endless flow of champagne. The traditional menu, however, has slipped, terrapin being replaced by pheasant or "something else." When I first went to the Assembly in 1939, terrapin was still being served. Never having tasted this stewlike dish of turtle meat served in a brownish paste, which outsiders seldom appreciate but Philadelphians adore, I wasn't as impressed by the menu as I was by the formality of having to curtsy to the ladies in the receiving line, among whom (another tradition) there was a bride of that year. I was also enchanted — and who would not be — by the sight of beautifully groomed couples waltzing, the men's tails flying out, the ladies' skirts billowing to a rhythm very seldom heard any more. One could sense that all these dancers were friends and relatives.

With few exceptions, the ladies wore real gems — many of them having gone to the bank to pick them out of their safe-deposit boxes for this grand *soirée*. Fortunately, my husband's aunt Harriet Brown felt so strongly about our attending the Ball that she presented me with the most valuable jewelry I've ever had — a double diamond pendant which I proudly wore that night for the first time.

The last and largest of the Main Line estates, still intact, and very much alive, is Ardrossan Farms in Villanova. At the beginning of the twentieth century, Colonel Robert Leaming Montgomery (he became a colonel during World War I) was fox hunting one morning, when his horse hit a fence and his tumble caused a momentary blackout. As the Colonel came to, he found himself in what he described as "sheer heaven." "Someday," he thought, "my house will be built right here on this hill." And sure enough, in 1909, he bought seven hundred and fifty acres, and the large house of Ardrossan sits on the very spot where he had once "seen stars."

While the Colonel was still alive, Emlen and I were often lucky enough to be invited there for the famous Montgomery Sunday night suppers. Their four children — Hope, Mary Binney, Alec, and Charlotte Ives (affectionately known as Floppette) were free to invite enough guests to fill the thirty-six chairs around the mahogany table in the huge walnut-paneled dining room. At either end of the table, Colonel and Mrs. Montgomery, in formal attire, would prepare the evening's delicacies in chafing dishes.

Mary Binney had been a piano soloist with the Philadelphia Orchestra when Leopold Stokowski was maestro *en résidence*, but she later turned to dancing and with her own group performed her own choreography of *Joseph and His Brethren* at the Summer Dell Concert Series in 1940.

It is mainly due to her sister Hope (Mrs Edgar Scott) that Ardrossan is still a working farm with some three hundred and fifty cows, all descended from Colonel Montgomery's original nine cows and a bull imported from Ayrshire in 1910. The office on the Ardrossan grounds is a two-story fieldstone farmhouse dating back to pre-Revolutionary times. "Every time I go into it," Hope says, "I can't help remembering that George Washington and Lafayette once had dinner together in this room."

Ardrossan's milk is sold to the Wawa Dairy Farms near Media owned by Hope's cousins, the Graham Woods, so the business is kept in the family in the true Philadelphia manner. In spite of this time-consuming dairy business, Hope is much better known as one of America's top-notch riders, fox hunters, and horse trainers. In the modernized farmhouse Orchard Lodge, also on the Ardrossan estate, shelves glitter with rows of silver cups won by Hope, the first woman to be invited to judge at the National Horse Show in Madison Square Garden.

Hope's husband, Edgar, a stockbroker, is Dean of the Shakespeare Society of Philadelphia and ex-President of the World Affairs Council and the Stock Exchange. He is the senior partner of the firm of Montgomery Scott, founded by his father-in-law, in which Edgar Scott, Jr., and Alexander Montgomery, Hope's brother, also work — which merges the families not only in marriage but in business.

CLANS AND FRIENDS

Philadelphians are more clanny than snobbish. They would rather spend their leisure time in the company of relatives and friends of long standing than risk spreading themselves thin with people who might never become part of their intimate circles.

Even more liberal hosts and hostesses who entertain theater people, artists, and out-of-towners will most likely surround their luminaries with a solid hedge of intimate friends. You never go to a party in Philadelphia without finding a predominance of guests who know one another, and usually very well.

The Edgar Scotts at Orchard Lodge have probably entertained as many celebrities as any Philadelphians, but they are, nevertheless, a closely knit family. I first met Edgar when I arrived in Boston from Florence. He was acting in Harvard's Cercle Français plays, with my sisters Berta and Francesca. In one of these, François Coppée's *Le Passant*, Edgar (as Zanetto) entered the garden of the courtesan (Berta Braggiotti), swept his plumed hat across his chest in a low bow, knelt before the lady, and strummed his guitar. My sister Marta and I, and Edgar's two sisters, Anna (Mrs. Moorhead Kennedy of New York) and Susie (Mrs. Alexander Wheeler of Bryn Mawr), bounced up and down in our seats, scarcely able to restrain ourselves from squealing with delight.

Years later, as a newlywed in Philadelphia, I was immediately drawn to Edgar's mother, Mrs. Edgar Scott, Sr. When Emlen took me to tea at Woodburne in Bryn Mawr, I remember being impressed by Mrs. Scott's aristocratic bearing, and by her exquisite living room with its eight Corot paintings, Degas sketches, and famous Manet portrait of Emilie Ambre. Mrs. Scott possessed a rare gift of inspiring good manners while encouraging her guests to express themselves without inhibition. If anyone present at her lunches, teas, or dinners played the piano, danced, sang, or recited, the stimulating atmosphere usually drew out an impromptu performance, just as it had with our family in Florence and in Boston. This atmosphere of self-expression was carried over to the Edgar Scotts' house, where I remember Beatrice Lillie getting up, with a dead-pan expression and a wink, to tell stories so excruciatingly funny we kept egging her to go on and on. Other stage people, who in New York seemed more difficult to communicate with, dropped their theatrical cloaks and appeared completely at home at the Scott *soirées*. When playing Philadelphia in Broadway-bound shows Gertrude Lawrence, Anita Loos, Helen Hayes, and other theatrical visitors always enjoyed themselves at the Scotts'.

When Philip Barry's *The Philadelphia Story* had its *première* in Philadelphia (with Katharine Hepburn as the star), Mr. and Mrs. Barry usually lunched with the Scotts on Sunday. Barry had dedicated his comedy about a Main Line debutante to Edgar and Hope, in whose company he had gleaned so much local color. One of the play's *jeux de mots*, "Qu'est-ce que c'est Cassatt?" has all the earmarks of Scott party conversation. A visit with Hope's parents, Colonel and Mrs. Robert Montgomery, could be equally lively.

A meal at the Yarnalls' in Devon with the family clan and friends (usually Sunday lunch) was also anything but dull. The four Yarnall children took after their nimble-witted father, Charlton, and often capped his speeches with amusing ones of their own. "I think our family love of performing most probably began early in our lives," explains Agnes, the sculptress and youngest of the Yarnall clan. "In our childhood we sat up at our parents' Sunday evening musicales, mainly chamber music, our favorite being the Rich quartet. It made us want to become performers ourselves." In those days the Yarnalls' winter house stood on the northeast corner of Seventeenth and Locust Streets — an area long since changed — and their big white summer house is now a nursing home.

Agnes and her husband Laurence Le Page, an inventor and the chairman of the Board of the Franklin Institute, carry on the family tradition of eloquent dinner speeches, especially on New Year's Eve, when as many Yarnalls as are available convene. Alec Yarnall died recently, but Marjorie (Mrs. Arthur Emlen Newbold) and Sophy Yarnall Jacobs, who now lives in New York, help Agnes to uphold the family traditions. One of Laurence Le Page's hobbies is assembling hi-fi recorders and amplifying systems which throughout most meals blast music nonstop — the louder the better, it would seem. Like all big families the Yarnalls are able to make sense through deafening interference.

Recently Agnes Yarnall completed a statue of Benjamin Franklin, commemorating the inventor's famous kite experiment. The statue has been permanently placed in Vincent Kling's new annex of the Franklin Institute Research Laboratories at Twentieth and Cherry Streets.

When you think about the Biddles, you think big. Groups of Biddles are scattered in and all around Philadelphia; some live on the Main Line, others in Chestnut Hill, and many of them in other parts of the world. No matter where they land, the Biddles manage to maintain their Philadelphia manner and special way of speaking.

In Philadelphia, the name Biddle is as indispensable as Lodge and Cabot are in Boston or Astor and Vanderbilt would be in New York. You could hardly live in this city without sooner or later being exposed to a Biddle, and, moreover, being glad of it. I have never met one of them who did not have friendly manners and exceptional charm. When you meet a new member of the clan you are inclined to feel you may have seen or met him or her before.

One might almost coin an adjective, and merely say, "He or she is so very Biddle."

Painter and author George Biddle, for instance, who has lived for many years in New York State at Croton-on-Hudson, has not lost his Biddle gloss, and neither has his attorney brother, Francis Biddle, probably the most celebrated of the clan. For many years Francis has lived in Washington with his wife, poetess Katherine Chapin Biddle (whose sister, Cornelia, sculptured the polished granite frog in Rittenhouse Square). During Franklin D. Roosevelt's administration, Francis Biddle was Attorney General, and more recently he was one of the judges at the Nuremberg trials. He is also the author of many books. Not even the brashest influences of a political career have tarnished the Biddle polish. Tall and wide-faced, he has an ever-ready smile, no matter how crushing the crowd or urgent the demand for his attention.

Equally attentive and considerate was the late Colonel Anthony Drexel Biddle. He was so warm and effusive that if you didn't know for sure how genuinely affectionate and kind he was, his flattery might have struck you as insincere. Mrs. Alexander Biddle says, "I have never known anyone who bubbled with a more genuine love of people than Tony — and I've known him since I was seventeen."

During World War II Anthony Drexel Biddle was Ambassador to Poland, and following that he was appointed as ambassador to governments in exile in London. His local mark was stamped during the years he served as Adjutant General of Pennsylvania, and when General Eisenhower was Supreme Commander overseas, Colonel Biddle was appointed as his aide. Finally, during the Kennedy Administration, he was Ambassador to Spain; his nephew, Angier Biddle Duke, has now followed him in this post. After starting out as the youngest envoy to El Salvador, Angier did not take long to rise to Chief of Protocol of the State Department, a post he holds with true Biddle zest.

His ebullient mother, the former Cordelia Biddle (Mrs. T. Markoe Robertson), is the author of *My Philadelphia Father*, which was made into the Broadway hit and Disney movie *The Happiest Millionaire*. Very much of a character, the elder Tony combined Biddle glamour with popular boxing, and trained marines in bayonet fighting and jujitsu during World War I. From all reports, he was equally daring in wild parlor games, which in no way detracted from his Biddle stature.

During the Philadelphia run of *The Happiest Millionaire* Walter Pidgeon had so absorbed the Biddle aura that at parties people often mistook him for a legitimate Biddle, a role he would sometimes carry off to perfection, just for the fun of it.

The magic of the Biddle name has also drifted to New York, where James Biddle was for a time curator of the American Wing at the Metropolitan Museum. He is now President of the National Trust for Historic Preservation in Washington. Jimmie and his wife, Louisa (daughter of Mr. and Mrs. Lammot du Pont Copeland of Greenville, Delaware), keep a firm foothold on Pennsylvania soil, bringing their children for weekends and for the summer to The Cottage, their house on the property of Jimmie's parents, Mr. and Mrs. Charles Biddle, whose Andalusia, one of the most famous houses in America, rises in Grecian grandeur above a vast lawn that sweeps down to the Delaware River near Bristol.

When Jimmie's great-great-grandfather, Nicholas Biddle, inherited Andalusia from his father-in-law, it was built in the late-eighteenth-century Federal style. As a young man Nicholas had traveled to Greece, and he always remained hypnotized by the beauty of Classic architecture. His dream was to revamp Andalusia into a columned mansion. Nicholas Biddle had been chairman of the committee for selecting an architect for Founder's Hall and other Girard College buildings. Architect Thomas Ustick Walter defeated his teacher William Strickland and Isaiah Rogers of Boston in the competition, and between 1833 and 1847 he completed one of the handsomest Greek-revival buildings in this country, if not in the world. Founder's Hall launched Walter's career, which culminated later in his design for the cast-iron dome of the Capitol in Washington, reminiscent of St. Paul's Cathedral in London. Nicholas Biddle commissioned Walter to remodel Andalusia as it is today, with its portico inspired by the Hephaisteion at Athens.

One summer's day Emlen and I visited Andalusia. Louisa Biddle cooked *fettuccine al burro* on the terrace, and after strolling through the Italian garden with its fountain and boxwood borders, we swam in the pool before Jimmie Biddle took us on a tour of the main house. In the marble-floored hall, the bust of Nicholas Biddle and his portrait by Sully made us feel quite aware of his presence.

We were shown an Empire bed which belonged to Napoleon's brother Joseph Bonaparte, and came from his house, Point Breeze, in Bordentown, not far from Andalusia. In the library was a volume of the Lewis and Clark diaries describing their first trip out West. The two explorers returned to Philadelphia with Indian artifacts and some live bear cubs which were put on view near Independence Hall to foster interest in America's expanding frontiers. Another curious item is a prospectus published by Lea and Blanchard for a Philadelphia magazine which was to have been edited by Edgar Allan Poe. In its back pages is a receipt showing that Nicholas Biddle had paid for a four-year advance subscription to help encourage this venture, which in the end never materialized.

Continuity of family name and of property is well perpetuated in Andalusia, and Jimmie's and Louisa's children are the fifth generation to be brought up there.

Another locally famous Biddle was the late Linford, a ruddy, fat, tweedy bachelor who was known to be able to eat a whole chicken with the gusto of Henry the Eighth, and in his old age was referred to as "Courtly Gaga." His father, Colonel Alexander Biddle, first brought curry powder to Philadelphia, and a brand labeled "Colonel Alexander Biddle's Original Formula for Indian Curry Powder" is still put up by a pharmacist, John P. Dooley, on the Bethlehem Pike. There are many stories about Linford Biddle, including the incident at his camp, Indian Point, near Bar Harbor where one day he discovered trespassers spreading their picnic baskets on his property. Polite but adamant, Linford demanded, "You know you are trespassing on my grounds?" The intruders promised to leave "as soon as we've finished eating — " but Linford declared: "I think that you will leave NOW," and he began undressing in front of the picnickers, to the particular consternation of the ladies.

Another story of unruffled dignity is told of Linford's brother, Louis, who went on a trip to the Middle East with Harry Lear and Anthony J. Drexel. When they reached Cairo, the two other *bon vivants* lost track of Biddle, and after hunting for him, discovered him in the small hours in a house of ill-repute. Recognizing his travel companions, Biddle rose to his feet majestically, albeit disheveled, and uttered his famous admonition: "Before you say a thing, gentlemen, I want you to know that these ladies are my friends. . . . "

The deeper you dig into Biddle family roots, the more branches blossom out. Most intimate to us are Mr. and Mrs. Alexander Biddle. He is the grandson of Colonel Alexander Biddle, and is the brother of three very attractive ladies: the late Mrs. John Penn Brock, the late Mrs. A. J. Drexel Paul, and the impeccable and witty Mrs. T. Charlton Henry, who lives at Eastdene, Chestnut Hill, and is always on the national list of "Best Dressed Women."

Once President of the Philadelphia Stock Exchange, Alec Biddle, tall and handsome in the manner of a Roman Emperor, is now retired, and lives with his vivacious wife, Margot, at Leighton House, in Bryn Mawr. It was partly remodeled and landscaped in 1928 by the famous Philadelphia architect, the late George Howe, who with William Lescaze built the impressive Philadelphia Saving Fund Society building.

Margot was the daughter of William Ellis Scull, a descendant of Nicholas Scull, surveyor for William Penn when he laid out the plan for Philadelphia.

"I am rather proud of this connection," Margot once said over a cup of tea in her elegant drawing room, with its Gilbert Stuart portrait of Washington, and then added with a chuckle, "I am also proud of the fact that my plain Quaker Scull ancestors settled in Philadelphia before the glamorous Biddles. . . . "

Margot is one of the last of Philadelphia's *salonnières*, encouraging all kinds of musical, theater, opera, and museum doings. Around her tea table the Le Pages, the Robert Strausz-Hupés, the Morton Howards, the Francis Boyers, the Rodolphe de Schauensees, the David

Biddles, and many more friends and relatives have gotten to know such artists as Ruth Draper, Lucretia Bori, and Cole Porter. There isn't a song the late Porter composed that Margot cannot play and sing without missing a lyric.

The names Biddle and Cadwalader in Philadelphia are as often linked together as are Lodge and Cabot in Boston, and serve as springboards for similar stories. "When a Biddle gets drunk he thinks he's a Cadwalader" is a favorite line, and the story about the moose in the Museum of Natural Sciences having been shot by a Biddle and stuffed by a Cadwalader has an enduring vigor.

The late Williams Biddle Cadwalader was the president of the zoo for many years, and it was during his administration that the new Lion House was inaugurated. Dr. Cadwalader and his late brother Lambert were two of the most charming men in Philadelphia. They combined "old school" manners with up-to-date interests, Lambert working for fourteen years in the State Legislature as Representative for Lower Merion. Emmie, his daughter, moved to Denver, Colorado after she married John Bunker, son of the Ambassador to Vietnam, Ellsworth Bunker. As an orientalist, Emmie greatly enriched the Denver Museum through the important role she played in acquiring a fine selection of oriental art, and in 1967 she received a Rockefeller grant to organize an exhibition for Asia House and the Museum of the University of Pennsylvania.

Emmie's first cousin, Christine Scull, who died only very recently, was also appreciated for her humor and her fearless repartee. She was a past master in Biddle-Cadwalader verbal skirmishes, and was responsible for the quip, "Biddles are better known for being in front of bars than in back of them." Once, when one of her oldest friends ribbed her for telling an "unladylike" joke at dinner, Christine, with a toss of her red head, snapped, "I don't have to be a lady — I'm a aristocrat."

Christine, who was safely embedded in an upper-crust Philadelphia background, loved to shock people, and a few years ago rocked the whole Main Line. When Brecon, the Sculls' brick Georgian house, had been completed by architect George B. Roberts, she commissioned Newton Harrison, student of Walter Stuempfig at the Academy of the Fine Arts, to create some statues to be placed at the front of the house. The work turned out to be a group of amorous couples cast in a plastic compound simulating bronze. The suggestive nudes, soon referred to as "those disgraceful figures" by the neighbors, triggered a bombardment of criticisms from church and civic groups that appeared not only in local publications but in the London *Times*.

As a result, the usually sparsely traveled County Line Road in front of the entrance was jammed with motorists out for a good look. Police had to be called to disperse the traffic and the Sculls were obliged to relegate the sculpture to the back of the house. Unruffled, Christine calmly commissioned another young artist to produce a less provocative group to replace the originals, and once again peace and quiet reigned in County Line Road.

Close family clans are the Atwater Kents and Emlen's cousins, the Lucases. Mrs. Kent (the former Mabel Lucas) has a brother, Brinton Lucas, who so resembled the late Ezio Pinza that he and his wife, Adelaide, could not resist going backstage to meet the male star of *South Pacific*. When the basso and Brinton caught their images in the dressing-room mirror, the astonishing likeness started a friendship that lasted until Pinza's death.

A. Atwater Kent's family came from Vermont, and the young inventor settled in Philadelphia, working in a small shop in the Society Hill section. After inventing the automobile self-starter named after him, he began making radios and amassed a fortune. Kent soon became a prominent member of Philadelphia's civic and social set. His wife remembers his factory in Queen Lane as being "more like a private house with nice furniture, soft rugs on the floor. The factory covered thirty-five acres surrounded by landscaped grounds. There were many facilities, including a tennis court and swimming pool for the employees, quite an innovation for those days."

All members of Cousin At's family owned at least one Atwater Kent radio, but his generosity went far beyond presenting sets to his friends and kin. Mrs. Kent's sister, Lenore Lucas, remembers one Christmas when nine or more Cadillac sedans were lined up along the driveway of West Hills, the Kents' Ardmore house, each a Christmas gift to one of his in-laws or cousins.

The Atwater Kent radio opera auditions in New York were one of Kent's most successful projects — an NBC program given every Sunday evening between eight and nine with guest stars from the Metropolitan Opera Company and other major companies. The purpose was to select young singers from every state to compete for five- and ten-thousand-dollar prizes which would further their vocal education. On one of these programs the great Frances Alda sang for the first time on the air.

Mr. Kent's contributions to Philadelphia have been many. He donated sixty-five thousand dollars for the restoration of the Betsy Ross House. In 1937 he saved the abandoned former Franklin Institute building and in 1938 opened it as the Atwater Kent Museum. With the aid of such civic-minded men as the late John Frederick Lewis, Jr., a great number of rare and important items of Philadelphia history were collected for the museum, including an extraordinary clock by David Rittenhouse, first American-born astronomer. Two other Rittenhouse clocks belong to the Drexel Institute and the Pennsylvania Hospital. Atwater Kent was also greatly influenced by Fiske Kimball, then Director of the Philadelphia Museum of Art, who emphasized the importance of displaying folk art and crafts. Joseph McCosker, the director of the Atwater Kent Museum since its inception, says, "We try to make the museum interesting to children since seventy per cent of our attendance comes from schools in New Jersey, Delaware, and Pennsylvania suburbs." Young people are fascinated by the shadow boxes, or dioramas, with animated figures telling the city's history, and by the collection of dolls, some dating back to the Civil War, many donated by Miss Mary K. Gibson and by Mrs. E. Florens Rivinus. Recently a maritime section has been added, with prints, paintings, and models — the section being a donation by A. Atwater Kent, Jr., now the museum's president. Atwater Jr., who looks startlingly like the Duke of Edinburgh, spends most of his time now in Palm Beach.

Intimate family friends probably associate the name Atwater Kent more with the great parties he and Mrs. Kent used to give. Life at their handsome estate, West Hills, was a lively, gay, and lavish affair, with champagne flowing and musicians playing, and sparkling entertainment. At one Kent party I remember dances by Ruth St. Denis and Ted Shawn, and songs by the Pickens sisters. Charlie Chaplin, Leslie Howard, Gladys Cooper, Helen Keller, Mary Roberts Rinehart, and the Kents' Kennebunkport neighbors, authors Booth Tarkington and Kenneth Roberts, were frequent West Hills guests.

By the 1930s a third generation of Kents and Lucases had swelled the family clan and there were never less than twenty for Sunday lunch at West Hills.

Before I married and came to Philadelphia the city was in the throes of lavish pre-

World War II parties. I remember Emlen speaking of the parties he had attended at White-marsh Hall, for Emlen was a friend and contemporary of Mr. and Mrs. Stotesbury's grand-children, Natalie, Frances, and Ned Hutchison, and he sometimes was their weekend guest. He remembers the movies in the basement theater, the champagne flowing, and the ubiquitous Meyer Davis orchestra. After a few glasses of champagne jolly Mr. Stotesbury liked to take over the baton. Mary Garden was a devoted friend of Mrs. Stotesbury's daughter, Mrs. Sydney Hutchinson, for whom she gave recitals in her house on Chestnut Street. Emlen told me that one night at Whitemarsh Hall, a printed pad was placed on his night table, with a complete questionnaire — from what he would like for breakfast to what time he wanted a car. The telephone had as many push buttons as a computer today, connecting with garages, greenhouses, gardens, pantry, and so on. Eyeshades were provided, and for novelty's sake he put them on. When he woke up the next morning he forget he was wearing them, and tripped and knocked over an inkwell, spilling ink all over the rug. He was so embarrassed he packed up and fled.

The trophy room in the house was filled with silver cups and blue ribbons. The salons downstairs were furnished with Louis XV furniture and Aubusson rugs, and the walls hung with Romney portraits, assembled by Lord Duveen to lend authority to the lavish interior. The mansion, designed by Jacques Auguste Gréber, still stands, but is no longer in family hands.

Philadelphians, particularly those in "the country," have always been known for their expansive way of entertaining even their relatives. Today there may not be as many big parties as there used to be, but the custom still prevails that the clans must gather at least several times a year for lunch or Sunday dinner; and how they *love* it — and how one loves them for it.

1

GLORIA BRAGGIOTTI ETTING'S ALBUM

2

3

I have always loved people and enjoyed entertaining and traveling. One of my closest companions has been my camera, which I carry with me almost everywhere I go. From the many pictures I have taken during my years in Philadelphia, I have selected for this album some candid shots of friends who are part of my life here — neighbors and visitors. Most of these were snapped at parties at our house in Philadelphia, a few at our summer cottage, Canaletto, at Loveladies Harbor, New Jersey, and others at the houses of friends in town and in the country. On the final page are a few of my photographs of celebrities who came to entertain servicemen at the Philadelphia Stage Door Canteen in 1945.

G. B. E.

4

1. Mrs. W. Laurence Le Page (sculptress Agnes Yarnall).
2. Dr. Georges Piguet of Lausanne and Mrs. Lawrence J. Richette.
3. Samuel Colt (son of Ethel Barrymore) and Mrs. Reeves Wetherill, being served by the late Miss Mary Heady, who worked thirty years for the Wetherills.
4. The late Mrs. Barclay Scull (formerly Christine Cadwalader) with Alfred Biddle.
5. Mrs. McFadden Ewing in front of Bloomfield, her château in Villanova.

↓5

1

2

3

4

5

6

7

8

9

10

1. Maestro Leopold Stokowski and Beatrice Lodge, now Mrs. Antonio de Oyarzabal.
2. Artist and author Ben Wolf and painter Edna Andrade at an artists' party.
3. Mr. and Mrs. Adrian Siegel in their house on Pine Street.
4. Countess Irene Cittadini.
5. Hobson Pittman in his studio at Bryn Mawr.
6. Nathan Rosenwald of the Savoy Steak Shoppe.
7. Mr. and Mrs. A. Atwater Kent, Jr.
8. Mrs. Brendan Walsh and Lee Nordness.
9. At the Emperor Restaurant: Mrs. John Franco of West Chester; owner Robert Maxwell, and Princess Sonia Doria.
10. Richardson Dilworth, President of the Board of Education and former Mayor.

1. Composer Samuel Barber on the grounds of his house, Capricorn, in Mount Kisco.
2. Edwin Wolf II.
3. Mrs. Matthew T. Moore, Chairman of the Philadelphia Art Alliance Dance Committee, and the late Leonard T. Beale.
4. Author Jerre Mangione with his wife, artist Patricia Mangione.
5. Pianist Rudolf Serkin, artist Andrew Wyeth, sculptor Wallace Kelly, and conductor Eugene Ormandy at the Philadelphia Museum.
6. William Bertolet, President of Bullard Antique Shop on Pine Street, Mrs. Josiah Marvel, and Manager Michael Logan.
7. Muralist Shirley Tattersfield and Mr. and Mrs. Joshua Logan at an opening night party.
8. Dr. and Mrs. Irvin Stein at Henry E. Gerstley's sixtieth birthday "opera" party.
9. Beatrice Lillie at the Edgar Scotts' in Villanova.

1   2   3   4

5   6   7

8   9

1

1. The James Biddles at Andalusia with their daughters, Letitia and Pamela.
2. Cecil Beaton.
3. Christine, hat checker at the Barclay Hotel for over thirty-five years, and Mario, the maître d'hôtel.
4. Noel Coward and Henry P. McIlhenny.
5. At the Charles G. Chaplins' in Haverford: Mrs. Avery Clark, Alexander B. Wheeler, Mrs. Igidio D'Ortona, wife of the Italian Ambassador to Washington, and the host.
6. Fashion designer Allie White.
7. William B. Warden, President of the Lyric Opera Company.
8. Concert pianist Jeanne Marie Darré and Sol Schoenbach, Director of the Settlement Music School.
9. Mrs. James Marcus, formerly Lily Lodge.

3

2

4

5

6

7

8

9

1

2

3

4

5

6

7

8

9

10

1. Princess Grace and Prince Rainier of Monaco at the Philadelphia Museum of Art. (Photo: *The Evening Bulletin.*)
2. Miss Juliet Stacks, teacher at Girard College.
3. At Leighton House in Bryn Mawr: Mr. and Mrs. Alexander Biddle and their son and daughter-in-law, Mr. and Mrs. David S. Biddle.
4. Actress Judith Anderson, concert pianist Thomas Brockman, and Andrew Seraphin, Public Relations Director of the Art Alliance.
5. Fiske Kimball, late Director of the Philadelphia Museum of Art.
6. Mrs. D. Chadwick Braggiotti and Walter Stait at Loveladies Harbor.
7. The late Major General A. J. Drexel Biddle. (Photo: U. S. Army)
8. Professor Robert Butman, Drama Director at Haverford College.
9. Françoise Gilot, author of *Life with Picasso.*
10. David J. Crownover, Executive Secretary of the University Museum.

1. Mrs. Paul Rosenbaum, Mrs. Rose Gimbel Stecker, Paul Rosenbaum, and Mr. and Mrs. William Loeb.
2. Mrs. Herbert C. Morris.
3. Artist Stella Drabkin.
4. Mrs. Eugene Ormandy with Orville Bullitt, former Chairman of the Board of the Philadelphia Orchestra, and Otis Wanton Balis, President of the Philadelphia Orchestra Association.
5. At Fairy Hill, Newtown Square house of Mrs. A. Atwater Kent: Mrs. Albert P. Francine, G. Brinton Lucas, Gordon Albert List.
6. Mrs. Gian Piero Nuti, wife of the former Italian Consul General and sister of Emilio Pucci, shopping in the Italian market.
7. Caskie Stinnett, editor of *Holiday* magazine, and Mrs. Peter Pulitzer of Palm Beach, creator of the Lilly dresses.
8. Mrs. Ira Haupt, editor of *Seventeen*, at the house of Mrs. Albert M. Greenfield in Germantown.

2

3

5

6

8

9

0

1. Artist Julian Levy teaches at the Pennsylvania Academy of the Fine Arts.
2. Mrs. Philemon Dickinson and Mrs. Brinton Lucas with Prentiss Kent at his birthday party.
3. Artist Marisol at Henry P. McIlhenny's.
4. Mrs. R. Livingston Sullivan (the former Timmy Lansing) and Mr. Sullivan, retired President of the Market Street National Bank, at their estate in Radnor.
5. Dinner at the Barclay: in the foreground from left, Mayor James H. J. Tate (then City Council President), Mrs. Richardson Dilworth, Sturgis R. Ingersoll, and Franklin C. Watkins (standing). From right to center: Mrs. Arthur Kauffman, Frederick R. Mann, and J. Lessing Rosenwald.
6. Tennessee Williams during the Philadelphia run of *Camino Real.*
7. Mr. and Mrs. John McShain. He is owner of the Barclay Hotel and former Ambassador to Ireland.
8. Simonetta Ailland and Jack L. Wolgin.
9. John S. Price, President of the America-Italy Society, and Stuart F. Louchheim, President of the Academy of Music.
10. Authors Glenway Wescott and Catherine Drinker Bowen.
11. Mrs. Robert E. Thomas, Mrs. Charles G. Chaplin, Mrs. George B. Roberts, and Mrs. Robert Strausz-Hupé, at the Chaplins'.

1. Samuel Adams Green, former Director of the Institute of Contemporary Art, and now Sculpture Consultant to the City of New York.
2. At the Ettings' thirty-fifth anniversary party for Mrs. Minnie Calhoun: James Davis at left; David Hallacy and Virgilio Franca dancing with ballerinas Provita and Florita Howard.
3. At the late Mrs. George S. Patterson's on DeLancey Place: Baron J. Maximilien de Schauensee, *Bulletin* music critic; Mrs. Alfred Kidder II, Mrs. G. Dawson Coleman, and Francis Boyer.

1

2

3

4

5

6

7

8

9

4. Frank P. Graham, Chief of the Education Division of the Philadelphia Museum of Art, at the George Chestons' in Wynnewood.
5. Marina Wister Dasburg, daughter of Owen Wister, with her artist husband, Andrew Dasburg, at Long House, Owen Wister's estate in Bryn Mawr.
6. Mr. and Mrs. George D. Widener at Mrs. Nancy Grace's in Haverford.
7. Mr. and Mrs. Henry Clifford.
8. Stuart F. Louchheim, Mrs. Francis Boyer, and Mrs. William A. Batt.
9. Mrs. Richard Rosenau as Salome at Henry E. Gerstley's "opera" party, with the host as John the Baptist.
10. Joseph X. Dever, Society Editor of the *Bulletin*.

10

1

2

3

4

5

6

7

8

9

1. Pierre Quilleret of Ardmore and Mrs. Robert M. Scott, at Mrs. Avery Clark's in Villanova.
2. Gonzalo C. Munoz of Chestnut Hill and Mrs. Rodolphe M. de Schauensee.
3. Henry E. Gerstley, President of the Settlement Music School.
4. At an art exhibition: Mrs. Alexander S. Kennedy and Miss Anna Warren Ingersoll.
5. Mr. Urban Moss III, real estate developer.
6. Madame Pierre Gabard, Dr. George Smiernow, and Mrs. Walter C. Pew at Mrs. Brendan Walsh's.
7. Mrs. Josiah Marvel of Eighth Street.
8. Architect George B. Roberts and Ruth Seltzer, Society Editor of the *Philadelphia Inquirer*.
9. Loelia, Duchess of Westminster, the guest of honor, and Anthony J. Drexel Paul at a dinner given by Mrs. T. Charlton Henry.
10. Architect Timothy Vreeland.

10

1

2

3

4

5

6

7

8

9

10

11

1. Mrs. Efrem Zimbalist. (Photo: Bradford Bachrach)
2. George Doan at Loveladies Harbor.
3. Fashion designer Ann Pakradoohi.
4. Former Governor of Connecticut John Davis Lodge, Mrs. Lodge (Francesca Braggiotti), and Professor Robert Strausz-Hupé.
5. Emlen Etting, Mrs. Emile C. Geyelin, President of the Alliance Française, Mrs. Rama Braggiotti, and author William Wright.
6. Joseph Pulitzer, Jr., of St. Louis, and Mrs. Pulitzer, the former Louise Vauclain of Haverford.
7. Walter Pidgeon, in Philadelphia for *The Happiest Millionaire*.
8. Author John Knowles.
9. Emlen Etting and Mrs. William Robbins, Jr., of Palm Beach.
10. Mrs. Stuart F. Louchheim, Mrs. Thomas Rayburn White, authoress, and Mrs. Samuel Rosenbaum (the former Edna Phillips), harpist with the Philadelphia Orchestra.
11. Mrs. Cortwright Wetherill and Reeves Wetherill at the Walter Annenbergs'.

1. Mrs. George Smiernow (composer-singer Anna Marly).
2. Henry Gardiner, Assistant Curator of Painting at the Philadelphia Museum of Art, and Mr. and Mrs. William P. Wood.
3. Mrs. Laurence Van Alen, Mrs. A. Atwater Kent, Mrs. Nicholas S. Ludington (Kassandra Van Alen), and Mrs. W. Perry Gresh.
4. J. Liddon Pennock.
5. Sculptor Henry Mitchell, Mrs. Robert Sherrod, Mrs. Livingston L. Biddle, and Mr. Robert Sherrod.
6. Mr. and Mrs. Samuel Chew.
7. Architect Louis I. Kahn. (Photo: *Philadelphia Inquirer*)
8. Mrs. Siegfried Roebling, Chairman of the Board of the Trenton Trust Company.
9. Mr. and Mrs. H. Gates Lloyd.
10. Artist-teacher James McWilliams.

1

2

3

4

5

6

7

8

9

10

1. Mrs. Donald W. McPhail in the Horticultural Society's garden.
2. Author Phillip Van Rensselaer and composer Charles Turner.
3. John T. Chew, H. Gates Lloyd III, and Mrs. Nancy Grace.
4. In Eugene Ormandy's dressing room at the Academy of Music: Mrs. Ormandy, Mrs. James Hatfield, and Ned Rorem.
5. Signora Luciolli, Signore Gianni Luciolli (Italian Consul General), Maria Callas, and Baron J. Maximilien de Schauensee.
6. Mrs. John Phillips, John Plant, Mrs. Cummins Catherwood, author John Phillips, Mrs. John Plant, and Mr. Catherwood.
7. Playwright William Marchant in his DeLancey Place apartment.
8. Mrs. Minnie Calhoun, who has been with the Etting family for thirty-five years.

1

2

3

4

5

6

7

8

1. Mr. and Mrs. Douglas J. Cooper, before their marriage, at a costume party.
2. Sculptor Rafael Sabatini and Mrs. Sabatini.
3. William Styx Wasserman.
4. Mr. and Mrs. John E. Canaday.
5. The late Jimmy Duffy, a Philadelphia institution, serving at a wedding party.
6. Mrs. Avery Clark of Villanova.
7. Samuel Chew, of Cliveden, Germantown, with Desmond Guinness, President of the Irish Georgian Society, and Mrs. Guinness.
8. Concert pianist Natalie Hinderas.
9. Mr. and Mrs. Ogden Nash.
10. Mr. and Mrs. George M. Cheston of Wynnewood.
11. George Balanchine, artistic advisor of the Pennsylvania Ballet Company.

1

2

3

4

5

6

7

8

9

10   11

1. Sir John Gielgud.
2. Artist James Kirk Merrick, Executive Director of the Art Alliance.
3. Mr. and Mrs. Georges Bernier of Paris, editors of *L'Oeil* magazine. Peggy Bernier is the daughter of Samuel Rosenbaum of Philadelphia.
4. Andy Warhol.
5. Miss Kay Halle, Nicolas Nabokoff, Mrs. Charles E. Bohlen (the former Avis Thayer, wife of the former United States Ambassador to Paris), and her daughter Avis.
6. Mrs. Lammot du Pont Copeland of Greenville, Delaware, and Mrs. Austin Lamont of Society Hill.
7. Gloria Braggiotti Etting with composer Gian Carlo Menotti and movie producer Neil Hartley.
8. Robert M. Scott, Master of the Ardrossan Beagles.
9. Mrs. Edgar Scott.
10. Poet Gerard Malanga.
11. Mrs. Franklin C. Watkins and artist Morris Graves.

1

2

3

4

5

6

7

8

9

10

11

1

2

3

4

5

6

7

8

9

1. The late E. E. Cummings.
2. Miss Gertrude Ely, of Bryn Mawr, with Dr. José Sozaya and the late Madame Paul Cret.
3. Mrs. Madison Clews of Malvern.
4. Designer Ludwig Ullmann.
5. Franklin C. Watkins at his seventieth birthday one-man show at the Philadelphia Museum of Art.
6. Mrs. William B. Warden of New Hope and Mrs. Frank Carano (wife of the Treasurer of the America Italy Society), with former Italian Consul General Gian Piero Nuti in the background.
7. Mrs. Walter H. Annenberg with Dimitri Shostakovitch.
8. The late William A. Batt and Philip Klein.
9. At the George M. Chestons': Henry Francis du Pont of Winterthur and Mrs. John Wintersteen, President of the Philadelphia Museum of Art.
10. Mrs. T. Charlton Henry.

10

1

2

3

4

5

6

7

8

9

10

11

1. Lady Sylvia Ashley, Helen Hayes, Mrs. Upton Favorite (President of the Stage Door Canteen), and the late Mrs. Dorothy Clark Norman.
2. Eleanor Roosevelt.
3. Mario Braggiotti.
4. Clare Boothe Luce.
5. Duke Ellington.
6. Alfred Lunt and Lynn Fontanne.
7. Gregor Piatigorsky.
8. Eddie Cantor.
9. Irene Castle.
10. Frank Sinatra.
11. Katharine Cornell.
12. Gertrude Lawrence.
13. Ruth Draper.
14. Antony Tudor, Agnes de Mille, and Lucia Chase.
15. Ilka Chase.

12

13

14

15

THE OLDEST
AND THE NEWEST

Most discussions about Philadelphia today start and end with Society Hill, one of the most well-known projects in city planning and urban renewal in the country. Unlike Virginia's Colonial Williamsburg and Massachusetts's Old Sturbridge Village, which are, in effect, museums, Society Hill is a restored city-within-a-city where people live in some of the country's oldest buildings, while enjoying every kind of modern convenience and the advantage of well-planned parks and walks.

In January 1962, Richardson Dilworth, then Mayor of Philadelphia, said, "I see a great city becoming even greater — I see our blighted areas yielding to new homes, to new parks, to sunlight, and to open air." These were not idle words delivered in a political vacuum; they were fighting words which he supported by building his own beautiful Colonial-style house in the disfigured area facing Washington Square, giving the Society Hill program its initial impetus.

A group of responsible men, all keenly interested in Philadelphia's architectural heritage, united their talents in bringing the oldest part of the city back to its former glory. As Society Hill was injected with new life, similar improvements were carried out in other parts of the city where ultramodern structures were designed and built to integrate with the old. As a result, new buildings have blossomed everywhere. Jefferson Hospital's complex at Tenth between Walnut and Locust streets, Louis Kahn's additions for the Moore Institute, and his Richardson Towers and Eero Saarinen's women's dormitories at the University of Pennsylvania are notable examples of this architectural renaissance. The new structure designed by Carroll, Grisdale, and Van Alen for the Library Company of Philadelphia, the synagogue of the Beth Sholom Congregation in Elkins Park designed by Frank Lloyd Wright, and the new Stock Exchange by Vincent Kling are other important contributions. An energetic committee headed by Stuart Louchheim does its part by continuing the annual piecemeal restoration of the Academy of Music.

Among the leaders of this twentieth-century band of pioneers were Jared Ingersoll; Judge Edwin Lewis; Edmund Bacon, Executive Director of the City Planning Commission; Gustave G. Amsterdam, attorney and chairman of the Redevelopment Authority; Michael von Moschzisker, *Evening Bulletin* columnist and attorney; Charles F. Peterson; and Arnold Nicholson, ex-editor of the *Saturday Evening Post*.

Society Hill was originally named after the "Society of Free Traders," a group that invested in William Penn's "Holy Experiment." This slice of land, a bluff by the edge of the river, at the foot of Pine Street, includes today approximately one square mile in which there are more eighteenth-century structures than in any other city in the United States.

When Philadelphia, like a star dropped from top billing, lost its role as the nation's capital, it lost some of its pride too, and historic buildings in this oldest section — many built in the eighteenth century and no longer used for their original purposes — were abandoned or turned into tenements. Gradually the whole neighborhood degenerated into slums, with ugly lofts and warehouses rising on either side of the ill-kept streets.

Today Society Hill has been so transformed that visitors who viewed it only a few years ago are spellbound by the work accomplished. "Houses of the eighteenth and nineteenth century, disgracefully falling apart and ready to fall into oblivion, are now the center of a new urban development on the river front," says Holmes Perkins, Dean of the School of Architecture of the University of Pennsylvania, who is delighted not only with what Philadelphia has done, but with what it plans to do along similar lines in the future.

It was fascinating to wander through the streets of Society Hill again recently with Will Chandlee of the Philadelphia Museum of Art's Education Department, who pointed out many of the recent developments and showed me the progress made with his own house on Spruce Street. Only a short while ago, Will's downstairs rooms were part of a rundown luncheonette; now the floor has been leveled and the area transformed into an elegant drawing room. A charming little garden (until recently a neglected lot) with a bubbling fountain adjoins the house. What Will Chandlee has done is typical of what others, emigrating to Society Hill, are doing. Very little property remains that has not been bought, and most is rapidly undergoing renovation. The streets themselves have been restored by the Philadelphia Redevelopment Authority, which has financed brick sidewalks, Colonial street lights, shaded walkways, small parks, fountains, and statues.

Between Third and Fourth Streets, on Willing's Alley, the courtyard of Old St. Joseph's (Philadelphia's oldest Catholic church) has been restored, and the yellow stained-glass windows have never seemed more resplendent than they do now. "No doubt General Washington, Lafayette, Samuel or John Adams, or any number of signers of the Declaration of Independence, came here at one time," Will said, "regardless of their religion." The Episcopal Community Services occupy another landmark, Old St. Paul's, and the Powel House (now open as a museum), where Colonial Mayor Samuel Powel and his wife, the former Elizabeth Willing, entertained Washington, Jefferson, and Adams, is close by. After attending one of Mayor Powel's functions, John Adams wrote to a friend: "A most sinful feast, everything which could delight the eye, or allure the taste, curds, creams, jellies, sweetmeats of various sorts, twenty sorts of tarts, fools, trifles, floating islands, whipped sillibubs, etc., etc. Parmesan cheese, punch, wine, port, beer, etc. — "

We also visited Carpenter's Hall with its famous cupola, and the gay Colonial Garden where a member-volunteer, Mrs. Donald W. McPhail of the Pennsylvania Horticultural Society, was busily weeding a flower bed. "We are going to plant more lantana, archeradium, and carnations," she volunteered. "We are doing everything we can to recapture the eighteenth-century flavor."

In complete contrast to the eighteenth-century architecture are I. M. Pei's three Society Hill Towers, which soar upward like exclamation marks, so well designed that they manage, somehow, to point up the Colonial past of Society Hill rather than to detract from its charm. Pei's monoliths remind us, cleverly, that twentieth-century architecture must take its place with the old through intelligent planning and design, and that this can be achieved excitingly.

At the base of the towers is a four-acre plaza decorated with flags and three bronze statues by Leonard Baskin. From the upper apartments, tenants have a panoramic view of all Philadelphia, Camden, the river, and the new marina.

On another occasion I visited Society Hill with Urban Moss of Van Arkel and Moss, the Philadelphia developers. "What we are trying to do here," Urban said, pointing to the restored colonnades of the market at Head House, "is to bring liveliness and an attractive atmosphere to the locale — a gas-lit square, intimate shops, a movie theater, bars, and places to dine. The place should jump at night." It had, in fact, already started to jump in the Head House Tavern, already in operation; and, more recently, Luigi's Restaurant; the Grape Arbor ice-cream parlor; and The Stuffed Mushroom, and Jeanne and Jeanine, two very French establishments.

Passing an empty lot with crumbling walls, Urban Moss said, "This will be a kind of Roman piazza — with a fountain and a double courtyard with rows of shops." Then he leapt onto the circular edge of a stone horse trough. "Drink, gentle beast," was inscribed on the side — with the date 1897. "We found this trough at the WSPCA at Broad Street and Hunting Park Avenue" he explained, "and we think it will make a terrific fountain." He jumped down and pointed at the low circular stone which acted as a saucer for the larger one. "See here . . . originally it was a dog trough."

Across from Head House (which dates back to 1802 and was so named because it stood at the head of the market stalls, on Second Street), several stores (including a quaint apothecary shop), are already well patronized. Eventually some sixty stores are expected to be in operation to serve the area.

The "millionaire's corner" of Society Hill is Spruce Street, where houses have been restored or newly built in Colonial and contemporary styles. Typical are red brick houses with traditional white trim, marble steps, and fanlight windows over handsome white doors.

A particularly lovely house on Spruce Street is the one owned by Henry and Anna Watts (he was head of the New York Stock Exchange), which is fondly nicknamed "The Embassy" and is located next door to the restored gem which belongs to the Jared Ingersolls. Much credit is due the Ingersolls for being among the very first to take an active interest in this historic area — before federal and state grants began to flow and the entire Society Hill project really began to blossom.

Other pioneers in this revived area are the Joseph Eastwicks, the James C. Crumlishes (he is a former District Attorney), who restored the Third Street house where Jacqueline Kennedy's great-grandfather, Michael Bouvier, lived, the Austin Lamonts, Frank Graham, Director of the Department of Education at the Philadelphia Art Museum, Robert Dyson, archaeologist-curator at the University Museum, and Bertha von Moschzisker, director of the Print Club. Among the newer arrivals is Nancy Grace, author of many children's books, who abandoned her house and pool in Haverford to settle in this new "old Philadelphia." Nancy Grace says, "I have always liked Society Hill because it seems to have more character than other parts of Philadelphia. . . . I think it is an expression of contemporary living within the oldest section of the city."

Much credit for the success of Society Hill must, of course, be handed to the federal and state governments and the National Park Service, as well as to the individuals who have purchased property.

"The great thing about this city planning is that the government was able to establish a set of conditions which has inspired purchasers to do their own restoring with their own initiative, their own resources, and, not least of all, their love," explained Edmund Bacon, executive director of the City Planning Commission. One of the reasons Ed Bacon (author of the book *Design of Cities*) considers Society Hill such a success is that "instead of our total restoration program turning into a series of museums you tiptoe through, it is a livable creation with deep and sensitive respect to the over-all image. . . . This thing, I assure you, has developed far beyond what I imagined. It is something that can only happen from the heart of the citizens for them to give their city a final richness."

The extraordinary work Ed Bacon has done in helping bring functional beauty to Philadelphia resulted in an invitation from President Johnson to be on the advisory committee of the Recreation and Natural Beauty Commission.

All our prominent citizens have something to say about the striking revitalization of our city. As Senator Joseph S. Clark has stated, "It was not the timid who made America nor did they make Philadelphia either. We of this generation in Philadelphia have a rendezvous with destiny as manifest as that of our forefathers."

Regarding the future of Philadelphia, the city planners tell us that they have the safety and comfort of its pedestrians in mind and project more landscaping and streets without traffic. At Penn's Landing a project is on foot for a mile-long green park with a yacht basin which will house, among many historic items, a replica of Penn's ship *Welcome*. These and many more projects are expected to be completed by 1976 — the year of Philadelphia's Bi-Centennial.

I fell in love with Philadelphia when I first saw it, and today I love it even more. When I think of Philadelphia thirty years ago, and of Philadelphia today, I have a wonderful feeling of continuity and progress. Although much has changed, the changes for the most part have been for the better. The best of the old traditions remain, and indeed, some of the very oldest, neglected for two centuries, have been brought back into sharp focus during this vital renaissance period. Philadelphia was, and it still is, a city of friends; it is a city with a glorious past and a bright future.